MW01147302

iDENTITY

IDENTITY

iDENTITY

WHO YOU

ARE

IN CHRIST

ERIC GEIGER

PUBLISHING GROUP

Nashville, Tennessee

978-0-8054-4689-0

Published by B&H Publishing Group
Nashville, Tennessee

Dewey Decimal Classification: 248.84
Subject Heading: CHRISTIAN LIFE \
SELF-PERCEPTION

5 6 7 8 9 10 • 20 19 18 17 16

For my daughter, Eden

While I wrote this book,
the picture of your ultrasound was on my desk.
And I already loved you.

Acknowledgments

I thank my wife, Kaye. While the world changes and ministry evolves, you are consistent in my life. You are my best friend, and I love you deeply. I cannot imagine life without you. Nor do I want to.

I am grateful for my family, my parents and brother. Eden is blessed to have you as Mimi, Pop, and Uncle Philip.

I am grateful for the team at B&H Publishing Group for their trust and encouragement.

I thank my pastor and friend, Rick Blackwood, who allows me to serve him and the church as his executive pastor. Each morning I wake up and wonder how two people are feeling: my wife and my pastor. I follow you, as I know you follow Christ.

I thank the staff at Christ Fellowship. Wow. God is amazing. And He is working among us. I love doing ministry with you. Specifically, I thank my phenomenal assistant, Sharon, who has served alongside me since I arrived in Miami.

I thank the people of Christ Fellowship throughout Miami. I identify with Paul, who told the church at Philippi that they were his joy (Phil. 4:1). Your commitment to aggressively advance the kingdom of God inspires me daily. Thanks for giving me permission to speak into your lives and tell your stories (special thanks to Pat).

While in this book I quote some people directly, my thinking has been shaped by a lot of preachers, teachers, musicians, and writers whom I have surrounded myself with over the years. We have never met, but I read and listen to you. So I thank Michael Card (*The Parable of Joy* is still my favorite book), Kenneth Boa (*Conformed to His Image* is a close second), Tony Evans, Joe Stowell, John Piper, Philip Yancey, Louie Gilgio, Caedmon's Call, and the Waiting (are you guys still alive?). If I hijacked any of your content in this book without crediting you, I am sorry. It was unintentional. In heaven I will apologize to any dead guys I forgot to credit.

In other words, I admit up front that I have few original thoughts. Even that statement is not original. Most of all, I am guilty of plagiarizing the Bible. I cannot help it; I love the Bible. And it is true. I cannot hold God's Word in me; it is like a fire that has to come out (Jer. 20:9).

See, there I go again. . . .

Contents

Contents

CHAPTER 1
||||||||||||||||||||||

Moving Forward

We cannot consistently behave
in ways that are different
from what we believe about ourselves.

—KENNETH BOA

I t is time to move on. It is time to move forward. I am not referring to a new job, a new address, a new relationship, or a new style of dress. It is time to move on in your faith. It is time to move forward in your relationship with God.

If not . . . then place the book back on the shelf. Don't buy it.

Maybe someone gave you the book, but you're not ready to move forward in your faith. Then fold the book a few times to give it that worn look and place it in the basket in your bathroom. Write the thank-you letter to your mom or your friend. But don't read the book. It will not be of much value to you.

Still reading?

Me too. And not only because I am writing.

I need to move on. Too often I stay in the same place spiritually. Too often I live on the truth of last month's devotional thoughts. Or the buzz of last year's mission trip. I keep talking about things God has shown me . . . years ago.

Is there nothing new?

Stuck?

I was asked to speak at a conference in Oahu. For the geographically challenged, Oahu is an island in Hawaii. After I prayed about it for 2.2 seconds, my response was, "Yes, Lord, send me." After all, someone has to go to Hawaii. And it might as well be me. Kaye, my wife, joined me, and we took a week of vacation around the speaking engagement.

We rented a car so we could drive around the island. The car was great, but each day we could not find the condo where we were staying. We would leave for the beach in the morning, but in the afternoon we were lost. The map was hard to understand, and the street signs were very confusing because each sign was filled with five or six vowels.

We knew how to drive to the condo from the airport. Those simple directions were given to us when we arrived. And finding the airport was easy because of the big road signs.

So each day we followed signs back to the airport and started over. Each day we would start from the same place as the previous day.

We wasted a ton of time. We were frustrated in airport traffic. And we felt like losers driving through the terminal each day. No doubt we looked a bit suspicious.

Finally, we had enough. We were tired of wasting time. We were tired of reliving the same scenario each day. We were tired of going through the same motions each afternoon. We were stuck. It was time to move on.

Do you ever feel the same way?

Perhaps you are stuck, spiritually speaking. Maybe you feel like you have not grown much since you began your faith journey. Maybe you have been going through the same motions for years. If so, you are probably tired of the same scenario. Nothing has really changed along the journey.

If you were honest, perhaps you would even call your faith boring.

Being stuck is frustrating. So much wasted time. Same daily grind. Perhaps you keep going back to the airport because that is all you know. If you are stuck, you are not alone. If you find yourself a bit bored or even disappointed with your faith, you are not alone. But it is time to press forward.

Pressing Forward

The apostle Paul continually pressed toward his goal of being mature in Christ. He admitted that he was far from the goal, but he kept moving forward:

> Not that I have already obtained all this
> [Christlikeness], or have already been made perfect,
> but I press on to take hold of that for which Christ
> Jesus took hold of me. Brothers, I do not consider
> myself yet to have taken hold of it. But one thing
> I do: Forgetting what is behind and straining
> toward what is ahead, I press on toward the goal
> to win the prize for which God has called me
> heavenward in Christ Jesus. (Phil. 3:12–14 NIV)

While Paul confessed he was not perfect, being stuck was not an option. He painted the picture of a runner who strained toward the goal. In other words, Paul assumed responsibility for his spiritual growth.

While Paul knew that God is the one who ultimately works in us (Phil. 2:13), he challenged Christians to partner with God in the process of becoming more like Christ. He told believers to "continue to work out your salvation with fear and trembling" (Phil. 2:12 NIV).

Work *out* your salvation. Not work *for* your salvation.

Salvation is a free gift given by God to those who trust and follow Christ; therefore, salvation cannot be earned. But once someone has received the gift of salvation, he is challenged to live it out, to mature, and to grow. The apostle Paul also wrote:

> Train yourself to be godly. For physical train-
> ing is of some value, but godliness has value for all
> things, holding promise for both the present life
> and the life to come. (1 Tim. 4:7–8 NIV)

Some modern and very loose translations could have, *Quit watching infomercials about spiritual exercise. Get off the couch and go for it.* The stakes are high. Moving forward in your faith brings blessing and fulfillment in this life and rewards in eternity.

Yet many of us stay in the same place spiritually. Despite God's clear instructions to press forward, many of us are stuck. We have heard sermons and read books on growing as a Christian, yet we are the same. We know there must be more.

Why are we still stuck in spiritual adolescence?

SPIRITUAL ADOLESCENCE

In the 1960s a social psychologist named Erik Erikson *really* developed a theory of development. He was not a biblical scholar or a theologian. He studied one aspect of God's general revelation: creation. He observed and studied people.

In Erikson's model, teenagers reach a point of developmental crisis. Erikson calls the crisis *role confusion* versus *identity.*[1] In other words, teenagers are searching for an identity. They want to discover who they are, apart from their parents. They want to be known for something, anything.

As someone who worked with teenagers for nearly a decade, I believe that Erikson's model has some credence. Teenagers are searching for an identity, a reputation. For many, a bad reputation is better than no reputation. They experiment with their dress, their music, their friends, their hobbies, even their walk, attempting to define who they are.

I remember one student as the poster child. Jonathan was searching frantically for his identity. One month he showed up to our student ministry meetings with baggy pants hanging dangerously low, big headphones bumping rap music, and a super-cool handshake that took twenty-seven seconds to execute.

Next month Jonathan arrived wearing jeans so tight that you could decipher the brand of tobacco in his back pocket. He talked with a twang and played country music with the windows rolled down. I looked for the big gun rack on the back of his truck but did not see one.

Evidently Jonathan's country-bumpkin identity did not suit him well either. A few months later he was dressed in all black, wearing some chains, and listening to people scream. He called it music.

Jonathan's constant evolution was interesting to observe but also sad. I would lay awake at night and pray, "God help him find his identity in You."

Erikson believed that if people do not establish a coherent sense of their own personal identity, they would struggle throughout their lives with relating to others and relating to the world around them. According to Erikson, if a teenager does not walk away from his adolescent years with a clear sense of who he is, he will never have a healthy personality.

He will be stuck. He will be continually confused about who he is. He will live the rest of his life wavering back and forth still searching for an identity. He will live in perpetual adolescence for the rest of his life.

Stuck as a teenager in an adult body.

Sadly, many Christians are stuck in an adolescent faith. And what is the reason for the entrapment? Why are so many Christians living in spiritual high school?

I believe the stagnancy is directly proportionate to the fact that most Christians do not know who they are. Most

Christians lack a coherent sense of who God has made them to be. Thus they wander through life merely existing instead of living the reality of who God has called them to be.

WHO ARE YOU?

Everyone searches for a clear identity. We long to possess a strong sense of who we are. And we crave to be known for something.

Some find their identity in their career. Working eighty hours a week is not working too much because the job is not only a job. The career is the person's identity. The career does more than pay the bills; it strokes the ego, pumps the daily grind with adrenaline, and provides feelings of accomplishment.

Others find their identity in relationships. Staying with him violates everything her conscience tells her. He is never going to propose. He treats her horribly, but she cannot walk away from the relationship. To be alone on Friday nights would be worse. At least she feels she belongs to someone. At least the relationship gives the perception to her friends and family that she is loved. Her identity is wrapped up in the relationship.

Some find their identity in possessions. The new car is more than a mode of transportation. *It is an expression of who I am. I just feel right behind the wheel.* He likes the way other people look at his car in traffic. In his mind they are looking at him. He carries a key chain with the emblem of his car to constantly remind him of his prized possession. He parks in the back of the lot under the light because a dent on his "ride" would be a blow to his identity.

Some find their identity in hobbies. Dressing up for the game with face paint and tailgating all day is more than fun. *It is my trademark.* Everyone expects him to wear the special tie on Friday's, the one with the team colors. And during the season he obliges. He memorizes the players' names and statistics, not only because he wants to know, but also because he likes to be asked. He feels good that he is known for something.

While careers, relationships, possessions, and hobbies are important aspects of our daily lives, they do not last forever. While God breathes purpose and meaning into the details of our lives, when we seek our identity in places other than Christ, we find ourselves empty.

So we have a choice. We can bounce from relationship to relationship, possession to possession, or career to career in a frustrating quest for our identity. Or we can embrace God's invitation to lose our lives and find our identity in Him (Mark 8:35–36). God invites us to a new and incredible identity. God invites us to find ourselves in Him.

And only in Him are we truly made whole.

The invitation to become a follower of Christ is also an invitation to a new identity. When you became a Christian, your identity changed. You have been made new through your relationship with Christ (2 Cor. 5:17). Your old life, your old identity is dead (Gal. 2:20).

To move beyond spiritual adolescence, we must understand who we really are in Christ. To move forward in our faith, we must discover or rediscover the identity that God has given us.

Rediscovering You

On the fourth day in Oahu, we committed to move forward. We refused to travel to the condo via the airport terminal. After a day on the beach, we pulled the car over and retrieved the map. Instead of taking another casual glance at the map, we dug into it determined to avoid the same routine.

After looking at the details of the map, we were able to locate exactly where we were. And we plotted a route back to the condo. Knowing where you are is critical.

Knowing *who* you are is critical.

It is time to take a closer look at the map. It is time to see what Scripture says about who you are. God is far from silent on the subject of your identity. The Bible is filled with phenomenal imagery describing your new identity as a follower of Christ.

While we will interact with many Scriptures in this book, the apostle Peter's reminder to Christians is particularly loaded with language about your identity:

> You are a chosen people, a royal priesthood,
> a holy nation, a people belonging to God, that you
> may declare the praises of him who called you out
> of darkness into his wonderful light. Once you
> were not a people, but now you are the people of
> God; once you had not received mercy, but now
> you have received mercy. Dear friends, I urge you,
> as aliens and strangers in the world, to abstain
> from sinful desires, which war against your soul.
> (1 Pet. 2:9–11 NIV)

Real quick, do something. Grab a pen and jot down the images used in the above verses to describe your new identity.

You are a . . .

Royal priesthood

Holy Nation

Aliens / Strangers

Using Peter's reminder as springboard for the rest of the book, we will interact with who God says you are.

- You are a child of God (chosen people).
- You are a priest (priest).
- You are His bride (holy).
- You are His servant (belonging to God).
- You are God's friend (people of God).
- You are an alien in this culture (alien and stranger).
- You are an ambassador (that you may declare).

As we understand who we are, we are enabled by God to live the reality of our identity. We are able to move forward in our journey with Christ. Embracing and understanding our identity in Christ impacts how we live, liberates us from performance-based Christianity, and honors God.

Identity Impacts Living

Freedom Writers is an awesome movie. Yes, I am a guy and just admitted in writing that I not only watched but also enjoyed the movie. It is one of those movies that when you tell your macho friends that you saw it, you preface the confession with, "I saw it on the airplane. It was the only thing playing."

Kind of like *The Notebook,* which I have not seen. I promise.

Freedom Writers is based on the true story of Erin Gruwell, played by Hillary Swank, and her freshman English class. Erin is a first-year teacher who is assigned to teach a group of students that the administration and other teachers have already written off as failures. Erin is told that the majority of the kids will drop out of school within the year and will live as thugs, gang members, and street kids.

The street is all they know. The street is just who they are.

Erin does not accept the gloomy prediction. Through creative approaches she gives the kids a larger picture of the world. She helps them envision a new identity. They are important. They have a voice. They can make a contribution.

As the students embrace a different identity, their behavior changes. They stay in school and their grades improve.

One touching scene in the movie occurs when a student returns after missing several days of school. He has been struggling with being pulled back into street life. He returns to school and has graded himself an "F" for his journal writing.

Erin pulls him outside of the classroom and hands him his journal. She challenges him to continue in his studies. He is not a failure. She says to him with belief in her eyes and conviction in her voice, "I see you. I see who you are."

I see you. I see who you are.

Her belief in him inspired him to keep going. She reminded him of his greater identity. She was able to convince her students that they had a greater identity than being street kids or gang members. They had something to say. They were writers.

And writers write. Together, they wrote a book. The book was published, and their story became a movie.

Our understanding of our identity impacts how we live each day. We live out who we believe we are. "We cannot consistently behave in ways that are different from what we believe about ourselves."[2]

God sees you. He sees who you are. And because He has given you a new identity, He expects you to live the reality of who you are.

- As a child of God, trust your perfect Father.
- As a priest, enter the presence of God anytime, anywhere.
- As His bride, live pure because He declares you pure.
- As His servant, serve gratefully.
- As God's friend, enjoy being with God.
- As an alien in this culture, live differently.
- As God's ambassador, represent Him in this world.

Identity Is Liberating

Attempting to live out our faith without first understanding our identity leads to a legalistic faith. Instead of enjoying the freedom that comes from a vibrant relationship with Christ, many Christians are handcuffed with performance-based Christianity. And the Christian life becomes a list of "have to's." You may have heard some of the list:

- I pray to God twice a day because I have to.
- I tell people about Christ because that is what I am supposed to do.
- I have to give so God will not have someone slash my tires while I am sleeping.
- I have to be nice . . . well, because I am a good Christian person.
- I have to buy peanut brittle from the church group at Wal-Mart.

Sadly, church leaders and pastors (myself included) have perpetuated the problem by neglecting to teach people *who* they are. Instead we offer pointers to people on *what* to do or *how* to live. It is much easier to teach and preach through lists of what people should do.

Do these things. Live this way.

While practical and application-oriented teaching is critical, we must be careful not to approach the faith as a way to act ourselves into a new identity. Instead of beginning with identity, we often begin with behavior. The order is wrong. Our identity must be the starting point. When we understand who we are, we are motivated to live the reality of who we are.

Jesus never intended for us to live with a list of "have to's."

The apostle Paul wrote to a group of Christians in Galatia who were trading in the joy of the Christian life for a legalistic pursuit of righteousness. His words are powerful; "It is for freedom that Christ has set us free. Stand firm, then, and do not let yourselves be burdened again by a yoke of slavery" (Gal. 5:1 NIV).

The day after Martin Luther King Jr. was assassinated, a schoolteacher in an all-white town in Iowa attempted to explain discrimination to her elementary students. The students could not understand why someone wanted to kill Dr. King.

The next day Jane Elliot came to class prepared to give her students a memorable experience on the pains of discrimination. She declared that the brown-eyed students were smarter than the blue-eyed students. The students with brown eyes were moved to the front of the classroom and given extra time at recess. The blue-eyed students were given special collars to wear so that everyone could see from a distance that they were inferior.

The next day Jane announced to the class that she was mistaken. The blue-eyed students were superior to the brown-eyed students. The blue-eyed students ripped off the collars with joy.

On the days when students wore the collars, they described feelings of sadness and inferiority. Academic performance was also affected. For example, when the blue-eyed students wore the collars, they needed 5.5 minutes to complete a reading exercise. When they were free from the dreaded collars, they completed the reading exercise in 2.5 minutes.[3]

While we are free in Christ, we often live as if we are collared with religious rules, rituals, and regulations.

You are free. Enjoy your freedom. Obey God from a grateful heart because He has set you free, not because you are checking items off a religious to-do list. Don't live with an enslaving list. In fact, because of your identity in Christ, your life is full of "get to's." *Not "have to's" or "mould do's"*

- As God's child, you *get to* know and trust your Father.
- As a priest, you actually *get to* spend time in the presence of God.
- As the bride, you *get to* be faithful to God.
- As God's servant, you *get to* serve Him.
- As God's friend, you *get to* hang out with God.
- As an alien in the world, you *get to* live for God's kingdom.
- As God's ambassador, you *get to* speak for Him.

Your Identity Honors God

Part of me was hesitant to write a book on our identity as Christians. I was afraid the content would be perceived as a pansy attempt to boost self-esteem. Honestly, a lot that is written on our identity in Christ is written from that perspective.

When I google "identity in Christ," I typically get pastel-colored Web pages with bad clip art and music. The Web pages give you a list of things to say to yourself.

Tell yourself you are this. When feeling sad, look in the mirror and read this aloud.

The approach reminds me of *Saturday Night Live* when I was a teenager. In the early 1990s, Al Franklen played a character on *SNL* named Stuart Smalley. The sketch was a constant jab at the entire self-help movement. Stuart closed each sketch by looking in the mirror and saying, "I am good enough. I am smart enough. And dog-gonnit, people like me."

The self-help movement has hijacked critical teaching on our identity in Christ. Many leaders have overreacted to the narcissism of the Christianized self-help section of Barnes & Noble by refusing to touch issues of identity. Sadly, the result is that many Christians fail to realize the greatness of their identity.

The end result of understanding your identity is not looking in the mirror and telling yourself how awesome you are. Nor is the end result of understanding your identity merely a happier you.

Your new identity is ultimately not about you.

Your identity is from God and results in God being glorified. The end result of understanding your identity is that Christ is praised. The end result of understanding who you are in Christ is that you will honor and glorify God.

Look again at the apostle Peter's reminder.

> You are a chosen people, a royal priesthood,
> a holy nation, a people belonging to God, *that you*
> *may declare the praises* of him who called you out
> of darkness into his wonderful light. (1 Pet. 2:9 NIV,
> emphasis added)

That you may declare the praises . . .

God is honored when you grasp who you are. Because when you really get it—when you really understand who God has made you—your automatic response is to declare how great God is.

Not how great you are.

Understanding your identity will impact how you live, will enable you to enjoy the freedom of your relationship with Christ, and will bring glory to God.

While God desires for you to enjoy life to the fullest, Satan seeks to steal, kill, and destroy (John 10:10). Satan does not want you to live the reality of your identity. Nor does he want you to live free. And he certainly does not desire to see Christ honored.

The Enemy's Scheme

Satan is your enemy, and he viciously attacks you. The Bible compares him to a roaring lion who prowls for the opportunity to devour you (1 Pet. 5:8). He seeks to destroy your understanding of your identity in Christ.

The book *Witnesses* discloses candid interviews with Jewish prisoners who survived Nazi concentration camps. Their stories are horrific. The goal of the Nazis was to destroy the identity of each person, to demoralize the prisoner.

The Nazis attacked the identity of each prisoner so that the prisoners would have no motivation to incite a rebellion. The prisoner would resign to live the remainder of his existence in misery. One prisoner named Walter recounts his story:

> Right after arriving to the concentration
> camp, we were herded into a room where all our
> civil clothes were taken off. We were shaved, all
> of our hair was removed, our bodily hair was
> removed. It went so fast, everything, and all the

work was done by other prisoners. See, the guards would stand by, but all the work was done by fellow prisoners. We took a shower and then I did get my number tattooed, which is 117022. This was supposed to be my name. I had no name anymore. That was it.[4]

No name anymore. A number. That was it.

The Nazis effectively distorted the identity of their Jewish prisoners. And the prisoners' lack of understanding about their identity caused them to live defeated. They were hampered from fighting back.

Satan attempts the same scheme with us. He attempts to destroy our understanding of who we are. He seeks to rob us of enjoying our identity as Christians. Sadly, he often succeeds. Because we do not understand our identity, we don't live the reality of who we are. We remain stuck in spiritual adolescence failing to approach life from the framework of our new identity in Christ.

Do not believe the lies of the enemy.

You are not a number. God has given you a phenomenal identity. You are His child, the priest, the bride of Christ, His servant, His friend, an alien, and God's ambassador.

You must understand who you are in Christ, or your growth will be stunted. Understanding your identity is the foundation to moving forward.

How to Read This Book

First, I want to be up front on the angle I am taking. I am not writing from the perspective of a biblical scholar or theologian. While I love the Scripture, I am far from

the expert. I woke one night terrified by the task of placing thoughts about God's Word on paper. *I say stupid stuff
all the time, and what if I write something stupid that will
forever follow me?*

I am a pastor. I love people, and I love seeing people
understand and live the greatness of our God-given identity.
While I am a pastor, I am writing from the perspective of
someone who is on the journey. I am proud to be a pastor,
but I find greater joy in my identity as a simple follower of
Jesus. In other words, I am more proud to be a Christian
than I am to be a pastor.

The thoughts, Scriptures, and stories on the following
pages are the overflow of several years of God continually
speaking to me through His Word about my identity in Him.
As I look over messages I teach, I realize I am continually
drawn to our new identity. Personally, God has used the
thoughts and Scriptures in the following chapters to transform my life. And I pray He will use this book to transform
yours.

I am writing as if you are already a Christian. The
chapters assume that you have committed your life to Christ.
If you are not yet a follower of Jesus, I am honored you are
reading these words. I hope that God will use the chapters
to give you a clearer picture of the life and identity you may
have in Christ.

Second, let me suggest that you not speed-read the
book in order to meet your quota of books read for the year.
Read one chapter at a time. Reflect on that aspect of your
identity for several days before you launch into the next
chapter. The first half of each chapter deals with a specific
aspect of your identity. The second half speaks to your
response. After all, our identity must impact how we live.

Third, if possible, read the book alongside others. As someone who lives in community with other people, I know God uses other people to help me grow. I am placing *Group Discussion* questions at the end of each core chapter.

Are you ready to understand your identity?

Are you ready to move forward?

Let's go. . . .

CHAPTER 2
|||||||||||||||||||||||||

You Are His Child
(Chosen people)

I will be a Father to you,
and you will be my sons and daughters,
says the Lord Almighty.

—2 CORINTHIANS 6:18 NIV

Adrian Greiner is a famous movie star, best known for playing Vince on the HBO series *Entourage*. Growing up in Brooklyn, Adrian struggled with the void of a fatherless home. In his early twenties he produced a documentary entitled *A Shot in the Dark* chronicling his search for his father. HBO aired the documentary in 2007, presenting the intense longing of a young man to connect with his father.

Good Charlotte is a popular alternative punk band. Two members of the band are brothers who grew up without their dad, and many of their songs are packed with deeply honest and heart-wrenching lyrics describing the pain of being abandoned by their father. One of their most popular songs, "Emotionless," echoes the words, "You broke your children for life" throughout the song.

You broke your children for life. . . .

As a pastor, I have counseled adults who still struggle deeply because of issues related to their father. Some struggle with issues of security because of a missing relationship. Others carry bitterness because of painful comments spoken decades before.

John's father left the home when John was a small child. John talks to him every few years on the phone for an awkward five minutes. While John tells his friends and family that everything is fine, he admits privately that he struggles. He struggles with self-confidence. He wrestles with his worth and identity. *What is wrong with me that my father did not want to know me? Does he think of me only every few years?*

Christy's father was a church and community leader to everyone else, but at home he was verbally and mentally abusive. She saw him beat her mother. She cannot remember hearing "I love you" from her father. She actually hates the word *father* now. She does not come to church much anymore because everyone calls God "Father," and she does not want another one. One father was one too many. Yet she admits she is empty.

Raul grew up in a single-parent home, his mother attempting to play both roles. She did a phenomenal job, worked very hard, and raised Raul right. He is grateful for his mother and feels guilty for wanting to find his father.

Raul does not want to disappoint or upset his mother with his search, but he has secretly been looking on the Internet for his father. He is not sure what he will do if he finds him. But he cannot stop looking.

Samantha's father is in prison. She is in elementary school, and I speak to her when I see her at church. She greets me with a hug. When the conversation ends, she reaches for another hug. Obviously, she misses the hugs of a father.

The pain created by absentee fathers points to the longing of all humanity for a relationship with a father. The bitterness over broken relationships with dads reveals the need for intimacy with a father.

There is a desire in all of us to love and be loved by our father.

And our Father.

The desire to connect with our father is a God-given desire and a reflection of our longing for God, the ultimate and perfect Father. Just as the absence of an earthly father creates a void, the absence of God leaves people empty. Augustine once wrote in his *Confessions*, "The thought of you [God] stirs man so deeply that he cannot be content unless he praises you because you made us for yourself and our hearts find no peace until they rest in you."[1]

Our hearts find no peace until they rest in our heavenly Father.

Another Father?

While we yearn for a relationship with both our father and Father, many people struggle with viewing God as a

Father. For many the word *father* is loaded with painful memories or the painful lack of memories. A plague of father-less homes, absentee dads, and lousy fathers impact millions of children and teenagers. More than twenty-four million children live apart from their biological father, and 31 percent of kids in America are being raised by single parents.[2]

Is it not obvious that the enemy, Satan, strategically and intentionally seeks to destroy fathers? Why does the enemy attack men and fathers so strongly?

Surely Satan realizes that by pulling fathers from their children he can twist their understanding of God as a Father. And if he can mess up our view of God, he can harm our desire to connect with God.

The enemy knows that God desires for you to view Him as Father.

Throughout the entire Bible, God is referred to as a Father. In the famous Sermon on the Mount—His first sermon to the masses—Jesus refers to God as Father more than any other title and clearly establishes God as a Dad.

Why does Jesus emphasize God as a Father? Why is it so important that we understand God to be our Father?

Many times people focus on one attribute of God to the exclusion of other attributes, which leads to an inaccurate view of God. But the image of God as a Father encompasses all of His attributes.

God as a Father encompasses His holiness because He demands respect and authentic worship (Mal. 1:6). God as a Father incorporates His great love (1 John 3:1), His goodness and generosity (Matt. 7:11), and His kindness as a Daddy (Rom. 8:15). God as a Father includes His sovereignty, as He is the authority over all things (Eph. 4:6), and His knowledge and wisdom (1 Pet. 1:2).

And God as Father embodies His justice as He disciplines His own (Heb. 12:7).

Maybe you think you don't want another father. *Been there, done that.* And you would rather do without. Yet God insists on calling Himself your Father. I love how Louie Giglio describes this tension: "God is not the reflection of your earthly father. He is the perfection of your earthly Father."[3]

God is not the supersized version of your dad. He is not just a blown-up replica of your earthly father. God is not your dad amplified in high definition and surround sound. Regardless of your earthly father's example, God is the perfect Father.

And He is your Father.

If you have trusted Him with your life and received Him as your Lord, He gave you the right to be His kid (John 1:12–13). Regardless of how you grew up, whether you had a great dad or a lousy deadbeat absentee father, whether you call someone on Father's Day or not, God is your perfect Father.

You are His child. You belong to Him.

The apostle John wrote, "How great is the love the Father has lavished on us, that we should be called children of God! And that is what we are!" (1 John 3:1 NIV). The word for "lavished" in the original language is in the perfect tense indicating that God's love is permanently fixed upon His children.

And that is what we are!

We have all been called names that are not true of our real identity. Just because the Atlanta Falcons call themselves a football team does not mean they are one. In college I called my friends dog. *What's up, dog?* They were not really dogs. I just called them dog.

But you are not just *called* a child of God. You are not the same person with a new label. You don't merely carry a biz card claiming you are a child of God. You have more than the title hanging on your door. You actually *are* a child of God, and God's love for you is great.

How great is the love the Father has lavished on you . . .

Why is God the perfect Father? What makes His love so great?

His Love Is Eternal

As I write this book, my wife is pregnant with our first child. Some people seem to get pregnant right away but not us. We tried for years to have a child and were told by doctors that it was highly unlikely. God continued to give us the desire so we prayed and begged Him to intervene.

And He did.

I will never forget when we discovered Kaye was pregnant. She woke me up early one morning to tell me a pregnancy test indicated a "positive." She cautioned me not to get too excited because the pregnancy tests were old, cheap, and without instructions. She hawked them off a friend and was not certain the line was strong enough to boldly proclaim she was pregnant.

My mind kicked into full gear with a plan. Like a good husband, I went to the bathroom with a different test stick to serve as a control group for Kaye's test. The line on my pregnancy test was very different than Kaye's, which was affirming news in more than one way.

After confirmation from our doctor, we called our parents to celebrate with them. I carried pictures of the ultrasound in my wallet. I was pumped for the privilege to be a father. I thanked God constantly for hearing our prayers. I put a baby countdown on my Google home page and longed for the day when the child would arrive.

After the doctor gave us the green light to tell people, we shared the news with anyone who would listen. When we discovered we were having a girl, we told our church that we were naming our daughter "Eden," like the garden.

One day a sweet elderly woman walked into my office claiming she was concerned. I sat back in my chair and braced myself for some critique of our church. She told me she was uneasy with the name "Eden" because it was not clearly a girl's name. I thanked her for feedback but assured her we loved the name.

The elderly woman's name is Pat.

Hmmmmm.

Obviously she did not watch the same *Saturday Night Live* episodes I watched growing up. After she left my office, I could not stop thinking of Eden. I realized that I was already defensive of her, already taking up for her name.

As I write this, I have not yet met Eden. She is still in Kaye's womb. I can feel her kick, and I talk to her, but her face and voice are still a mystery to me. Before she is born, I love her. While she is in the womb, I am proud to be her dad.

Your Father has always loved you. His love for you is eternal.

Before the world was even created, God knew you as His child. He permanently fixed His love on you from the beginning of time (Eph. 1:4). He knew that you would commit to follow Him and be born again into His family.

Your Father has always loved you and always will. Nothing will ever separate you from Him:

> For I am persuaded that neither death nor
> life, nor angels nor rulers, nor things present, nor
> things to come, nor powers, nor height, nor depth,
> nor any other created thing will have the power to
> separate us from the love of God that is in Christ
> Jesus our Lord! (Rom. 8:38–39)

No tragedy will take Him from you. You won't come home from school one day to learn He has left. He is not going anywhere. His love for you, as His child, is fixed and secure.

How great is the love the Father has lavished on you. . . .

His Love Is Personal

I cannot wait to be involved with Eden, to spend time with her. On the way to work, I think of my daughter. At times I pretend she is riding with me to her basketball (or ballet) practice. I listen to her tell me about her day and answer questions she has about mine. My mind wanders during meetings as I imagine holding Eden and tucking her in bed at night.

Kaye worries that I am going to spoil her. She is probably right, but I am eager for the relationship with my daughter.

Your Father not only loves you; He also likes you. He enjoys you. He delights in you and rejoices over you with singing (Zeph. 3:17). He did more than say He loved you. He proved His love by sacrificially dying for you, to erase your sins and establish a Father-child relationship with you (Rom. 5:8).

Even when Jesus taught His disciples how to pray, He emphasized the intimacy of the Father-child relationship. He told His disciples,

> This, then, is how you should pray: "Our *Father* in heaven, hallowed be your name, your kingdom come, your will be done on earth as it is in heaven. Give us today our daily bread. Forgive us our debts, as we also have forgiven our debtors. And lead us not into temptation, but deliver us from the evil one." (Matt. 6:9–13 NIV)

Jesus spoke Aramaic, and the word for "Father" in Aramaic is *Abba*, which literally means "Daddy." The Father-child relationship is the foundation for the entire prayer: *Daddy, Your name is holy. Daddy, Your kingdom come and Your will be done. Daddy, provide for me. Daddy, forgive me. Daddy, guide me and protect me.*

Your Father is not aloof, nor does He love you from afar. He loves you personally and extravagantly. He knows you by name and is an involved Father.

How great is the love the Father has lavished on you. . . .

His Love Is Intentional

While we often speak in terms of "falling in love" with someone, God did not fall in love with you. His love for you did not catch Him off guard or by surprise. He did not just happen to notice you one day and fall "head over heels in love with you." His love for you is intentional as He has chosen to set His great love on you.

Thus He will not "fall out of love" with you.

God uses the image of adoption throughout Scripture to drive home the point that He intentionally lavished His love on you (Eph. 1:5). You were not a "surprise" or an "accidental" birth. He was not disappointed or overwhelmed when you were born into His family. God was fully prepared to be your Father because He adopted you.

Adoption is beautiful because it is a picture of God's grace toward us. My niece and nephew, Gracie and Zachary, were adopted out of foster care. Bill and Angela (my wife's brother and his wife) chose to love Gracie and Zachary. They took them home as their own, assumed full responsibility for them, gave them rooms in the house and seats at the table.

Gracie and Zachary have been made family by grace. Their grandparents and aunts and uncles view them as full members of the family. I keep referring to "the family" as if we are in a scene from the *Godfather*. Kaye is the youngest of five kids, and all the other children live on the land. I describe the land as the family compound. When the Godfather (Mr. Billy Kennedy) speaks, everyone listens.

But Gracie and Zachary are not simply treated like family, like Tom Hagen in the *Godfather*. They are family. In fact, Zachary is the only grandchild who will carry the Kennedy name to the next generation.

The story of Mephibosheth is similar and illustrates God's intentional love (2 Sam. 9). Try to say Mephibosheth three times quickly.

Mephibosheth's story begins with David. David is the new king of God's people, Israel. As king, he could have executed the household and the servants of the previous king. Saul was the former king, and Saul hated David. He was jealous of David. The trouble that Saul caused David could have further justified David's decision to eliminate any remnant from Saul's household.

Yet David chooses to intentionally offer mercy and grace. He asks if there is anyone left to whom he can show kindness. He hears that there is this one person— Mephibosheth.

But he is crippled in both feet.

In other words, Mephibosheth will not be of much use. He will not be able to help out around the palace or in the fields because he has a severe handicap.

Mephibosheth is summoned to David. He comes shaking, expecting to be killed. David assures him that he has nothing to fear.

David gives Mephibosheth his family's land back. The land now belonged to David, yet David freely restores it to Mephibosheth. And he does even more. He invites Mephibosheth to "always eat at my table" (2 Sam. 9:7 NIV). This guy who deserved death, who was penniless, who could be of very little use to the king, was invited to sit at the king's table . . . *always.*

David adopted Mephibosheth into his family.

You are Mephibosheth.

You were crippled by sin, and you deserved death. Yet God has given you a new life by adopting you. Just as David searched for Mephibosheth, God searched for you. Just as David gave Mephibosheth a place at his table, God invited you into His family. Just as David assumed responsibility for

Mephibosheth, God assumed responsibility for you. Just as David intentionally offered mercy, God intentionally offered mercy to you.

How great is the love the Father has lavished on you. . . .

His Love Is Unconditional

As your Father, God loves you unconditionally. While many people love you *because* or love you *if*, God loves you *period*. Because of His unconditional love, your Father is merciful toward you (Luke 6:36). Instead of using His wrath and judgment to compel us to follow, He draws us through His mercy and forgiveness. The kindness and gentleness of the Father lead us to repentance (Rom. 2:4).

Jesus told a story about the Father's unconditional love (Luke 15). In the story, a son goes to his dad and wants to cash out with his inheritance. The son has some nerve asking for his inheritance while his dad is still alive, but the dad chooses to give his son his portion. The son leaves with the money and moves to Miami, Las Vegas, or New Orleans to party.

Eventually the money runs out, and the son finds a job feeding pigs. In the Jewish culture (the crowd who first heard this story), working with pigs was undignified and uncouth. The son is so broke and hungry that he desires to eat the pig's food. He is utterly miserable.

Life away from the Father always leaves us miserable.

One day the son comes to his senses and dreams of his father's home. *The servants in my father's household live better than this.*

Humbly he journeys home. Since all the money is gone, he intends to be a servant for his father. He will cut the grass, feed the animals, wash the dishes, and live in the servants' quarters. The son approaches his father's house with a rehearsed speech, asking to be a servant.

The father is home. He never left. During his day he keeps a hopeful watch on the road wishing his son would appear. *Perhaps this will be the day my son will come home.* And on this day the son's silhouette becomes visible from a long way off. The father recognizes his son. The father runs to his son, hugs him, and kisses him.

The son launches into his rehearsed speech, but his father interrupts him. He does not scold him for wasting his money or breaking his mother's heart. He does not yell at him to get cleaned up before he comes around again.

Instead, he throws a party. He clothes him with the best robe and places a ring on his finger, distinguishing him as a son with privilege and authority. The father brings sandals for his son because only slaves walked barefoot. And the father instructs the best calf to be killed so they may enjoy a celebration feast together.

Jesus told the story about your Father.

His love for you is unconditional; He offers mercy even when you drift away from the Father's house and waste all He has given you. He offers mercy to you every time you come home.

My story is similar to the story Jesus told.

I was raised in a Christian home with two godly parents, but the faith did not take root in my life. I attended church and would say I was a Christian, but I was too self-consumed to pursue a relationship with God.

At the end of my junior year in high school, I was arrested on multiple charges. Late one night a couple of friends and I broke into a guy's vehicle, stole his credit cards, and went throughout the city buying beer, Fruity Pebbles, and other essentials. The video cameras captured our image, and the cops matched us to the theft.

It was the most miserable summer as life seemed to crumble around me. I was one of the few guys in my class given the honor to attend Boys State (a leadership conference) but was uninvited after the arrest. My girlfriend's parents understandably did not want me to hang out with their daughter. I was the vice president of Fellowship of Christian Athletes at my school because I played hoops and went to church, but I was removed from my position after our arrest hit the papers.

My father came into my room one night after the arrest.

I braced myself for a biblical beat down, but my father calmly sat and opened his Bible. He read me some Scriptures and told me, "There is nothing you will ever do that will stop me from loving you." I never saw my father cry before he spoke those words to me. He calmly walked out of my room.

And my life has never been the same.

The unconditional love of my father pointed me to the unconditional love of my Father. God used the arrest and the heart of my dad to bring me to Himself. I was dead in my sins, but God, who is rich in mercy, made me alive in Christ (Eph. 2:4–5).

Your Father is rich in mercy. In fact, His mercies never end and are new each day (Lam. 3:22–23). He is always approachable. He is always eager to forgive. He is always ready for you to come home to Him. His love is unconditional.

How great is the love the Father has lavished on you. . . .

His Love Is Generous

My perspective changed when I learned I would be a dad. Immediately I assumed responsibility for my daughter, to provide for her.

Every purchase is made in light of our responsibility for Eden. I think of how to help pay for Eden's college, just in case she does not land the scholarship my wife is banking on. In the past extra money from speaking was earmarked "vacation fund," but now I think of Eden's future first.

I assume responsibility for my daughter, and your Father assumes responsibility for you. He is your provider. While establishing God as a Father in His Sermon on the Mount, Jesus spoke of His providing love for you:

> Therefore I tell you, do not worry about your
> life, what you will eat or drink; or about your body,
> what you will wear. Is not life more important than
> food, and the body more important than clothes?
> Look at the birds of the air; they do not sow or
> reap or store away in barns, and yet your heavenly
> Father feeds them. Are you not much more valu-
> able than they? (Matt. 6:25–26 NIV)

Your Father is an able and generous provider. He owns the entire world and everything is under His control. As your Father, He promises to meet all of your needs according to His riches (Phil. 4:19). And anything good in your life ultimately comes from Him (James 1:17).

Just as earthly fathers seek to be generous to their children, your Father is generous to you. Jesus continued describing the Father's heart for you:

> Which of you, if his son asks for bread, will give him a stone? Or if he asks for a fish, will give him a snake? If you, then, though you are evil, know how to give good gifts to your children, how much more will your Father in heaven give good gifts to those who ask him! (Matt. 7:9–11 NIV)

God's generosity was demonstrated in the gift of His one and only Son for you (John 3:16). God gave His only child so you could become His child. God orchestrated the cruel and sacrificial death of His only Son so you could live forever.

And His generosity continues. Not only are your sins forgiven through the death of Christ, but your Father has also declared you an heir to His inheritance:

> You received the Spirit of sonship. And by him we cry "*Abba*, Father." The Spirit himself testifies with our spirit that we are God's children. Now if we are children, then we are heirs—heirs of God and co-heirs with Christ. (Rom. 8:15–17 NIV)

While earthly inheritances corrode and dissolve in time, your inheritance will never spoil or fade (1 Pet. 1:4). Your inheritance will always be new. Since you are His child, He has generously given you life forever in eternal paradise.

How great is the love the Father has lavished on you. . . .

His Love Is Purifying

Your Father's greatest desire for you is that you would be like Him, that you would be holy. He cares more about your transformation than your happiness, more about your spiritual maturity than your comfort. Since He desires to conform you to the image of Christ, He will use every situation and circumstance to purify you.

In other words, your Father invented tough love.

When children fail to obey, good parents discipline. My parents were good parents. My father's weapon of choice was his belt. He would snap it together to let me know what was coming. He tried a pool stick once but reverted to his trusted belt. My mother preferred her cutting board as it fit well in her hand. There is no need to call Family Services on my parents; I appreciate their discipline.

Well, now I do.

Their discipline proved their love for me. Discipline is an expression of love, not the antithesis of love. Your Father disciplines you out of His great love for you. He does not beat you, but He does discipline you as you move away from Him. The Father's discipline proves you are really His child and pulls you back to Him.

Endure hardship as discipline; God is treating you as sons. For what son is not disciplined by his father? If you are not disciplined (and everyone undergoes discipline), then you are illegitimate children and not true sons. Moreover, we have all had human fathers who disciplined us and we respected them for it. How much more should we submit to the Father of our spirits and live! Our fathers disciplined us for a little while as they thought best; but God disciplines us for our good, that we may share in his holiness. No discipline seems pleasant at the time, but painful. Later on, however, it produces a harvest of righteousness and peace for those who have been trained by it. (Heb. 12:7–11 NIV)

Because your Father wants the best for you, His tough love is always for your good. His discipline purifies your faith. He has high hopes for you, and He has the ability to use any situation for your good (Rom. 8:28).

How great is the love the Father has lavished on you?

Your Father's love is eternal, personal, intentional, unconditional, generous, and purifying. You are His child. How should you respond to this reality? Living the reality of your identity as a child means trusting, obeying, and reflecting your Father.

1. TRUST

Jesus utilized children as an object lesson for true faith. He told the crowd of adults that they must become like children to enter the kingdom of heaven (Matt. 18:2–3). What was His point? What was He suggesting?

Children are extremely trusting, often too trusting. When Jesus invited children to come to Him, they eagerly approached Him. They trusted Him completely. Our response to Jesus must be the same. As your Father, He asks us to trust Him with all that we are, with every bit of our existence (Prov. 3:5–6). In fact, it is impossible to please God without faith (Heb. 11:6).

But faith is often difficult. Trust is a challenge. We prefer to be in the driver's seat of our lives. Is this why we feel safer in cars than planes despite the evidence that more people are killed in car accidents than plane crashes?

Physically I prefer to be in the driver's seat. I would rather be the one holding the steering wheel; therefore, flying is not my favorite way to spend a morning or afternoon.

During one flight aboard US Scareway, I thought I was going to die. I was in a little puddle jumper prop plane going from Cincinnati to Detroit, a plane that flies out of a concourse that you did not know existed and has teenagers for pilots.

Somewhere over the great Midwest, the plane started to shake violently. It dropped real fast. People in front of me were laughing but not with a joyous laugh. It was more of a horror-movie, eerie type of laughter. The lady behind me was yelling. I heard some crying. I was admitting to God that I was an idiot for boarding a plane that could have been used in World War I.

The horror only lasted for a few minutes. Once we smoothed out, I realized I was curled up into a fetal position next to this lady who was my mom's age. She was surprised. I was embarrassed. I assume that in the midst of the crisis, I reverted back to my childhood and was seeking comfort from my mommy.

Oddly, I have experienced worse turbulence in boats and cars than I did in the airplane ride from hell. Traveling in boats off the Miami shoreline and vehicles in Miami traffic provide a rougher ride but do not frighten me. When I am in a car or a boat, I am in control. Or at least I feel like

I am. On an airplane I have no control. I don't even see the pilot. Only occasionally do I hear his voice.

We struggle to release control. We struggle with handing the wheel to someone else to steer our lives. And our Father insists that we trust Him completely. He desires to pilot our lives, every aspect of who we are.

Do you trust your Father with every aspect of your life?

Your Father is trustworthy. While pilots are flawed, He is perfect. While pilots remain in the cockpit and rarely talk to you, your Father is highly involved in your life.

He can be trusted with every aspect of your life: your career, relationships, finances, and hobbies. Your Father does not desire to be merely included in your life, to occupy one compartment of your life. He seeks to take complete control. In fact, He brings meaning and significance to every detail of your existence.

And there is no one better to steer and pilot your life than your Father.

2. OBEY

Imagine a teenager is asked by his parents to take the trash out on the eve of trash day. It is 7:30 when the first request is made. The teenager is on the computer listening to his downloaded music, instant messaging a few friends, and amazingly doing homework at the same time. At 8:30, the teenager is reminded about the trash.

All the baskets need to be emptied, not just the one in the kitchen.

In a minute, dannnnnnnngggggggg. I am doing my homework.

At 9:15, the reminder is more firm: *Take out the trash now.*

Fine. The only reason you brought me into this world was to make me do chores. The teenager stomps around the house, breathing deeply, making as much noise as possible. The teenager slams the door as he comes back inside the house.

Obedience?

Obedience is more than doing the right things. Obedience flows from a pure heart and involves sincere motivation. Your Father looks deeper than the action. Your Father is concerned with your heart. "This is love for God, to obey his commands. And his commands are not burdensome" (1 John 5:3 NIV).

His commands are not burdensome when we view Him as a Father instead of a militant general who barks out commands. His commands are not burdensome when we first enjoy the Father-child relationship. His commands are not burdensome when we trust our Father and are grateful for His wisdom and constant involvement in our lives.

Are your Father's commands burdensome to you, or are you eager to obey Him because you trust Him fully with your entire life?

STEP 3. REFLECT

As a former youth pastor, I learned what makes parents proud. Parents love to hear how their children reflect them . . .

He looks so much like you.
She has your eyes.
She has your intelligence.

He has your business savvy.
She definitely has your athletic ability.
I see you in him every time I look at him.
The apple did not fall far from the tree with her
  personality.

We reflect attributes of our parents for reasons of both nature and nurture. Many of our characteristics are genetic and hereditary (nature). We also become more like our parents in time, as we are impacted by their example (nurture).

In the same way, you reflect your Father's attributes because of nature and nurture. When you became a Christian, the Bible says you were born again (John 3:3). God gave you a new nature, His nature. While you still struggle with sin because you live in an earthly body, you have been changed into a new person internally. And you no longer continually live in sin.

In fact, the Scripture explicitly says that God's seed ("sperm" in the original language) lives in you. "No one who is born of God will continue to sin, because God's seed remains in him; he cannot go on sinning because he has been born of God" (1 John 3:9 NIV).

The DNA test is clear. You belong to God. The evidence is that you do not continually live a life of sin.

As God's child, God nurtures you and develops your character. He continually molds you and forms you. He transforms your mind (Rom. 12:2) and works in your life (Phil. 2:13) so you will live out your identity as His child.

Your Father demands and desires for you to reflect His name and nature. He is pleased and proud when you reflect His attributes to the world around you. While you will never be perfect on this earth, you are instructed to imitate Christ and reflect your Father's character.

- Be holy as He is holy (1 Pet. 1:16).
- Forgive as Christ forgave you (Col. 3:13).
- Accept others as Christ accepted you (Rom. 15:7).
- Be merciful as your Father is merciful (Luke 6:36).
- Live a life of love just as Christ loved us (Eph. 5:2).
- Live in the light, as your Father is Light (1 John 1:7).

As His child, you have received His nature and nurture. He has called you to Himself and has named you His child. Now live worthy of the calling you have received by reflecting His character to the world around you.

The reality: You are God's child. He has lavished His great love on you.

The response: Trust. Obey. And reflect His nature.

Group Discussion Questions

1. How did your relationship with your earthly father prepare you for a relationship with your heavenly Father?

2. As a group, make a list of how the adoption of a child is similar to salvation.

3. Read 1 John 3:1 as a group. This chapter discussed the greatness of God's love for His children (eternal, personal, intentional, unconditional,

generous, and purifying). Which aspect of God's
great love meant the most to you and why?

Unconditional, I take comfort in that.

4. Can you describe a time in your life when God
disciplined you? How did the discipline result in
your holiness? *Yes, it shared me my motive is more important than my actions.*

5. Read Luke 15 together as a group. Read the story
not from the perspective of the son but from
the perspective of the father. Write down the
characteristics of the father in the story.

- Hopeful   - Unconditionally loving
- Forgiving

6. What are the attributes of your heavenly Father
that are most difficult to reflect to the world
around you?

Hopeful

CHAPTER 3
||||||||||||||||||||||||

You Are the Priest

(priest)

You are a . . . royal priesthood.

—1 PETER 2:9

W hat would tomorrow be like if you realized you are a priest? What would be different in the morning? How would the drive to work or throughout town change? How would you approach the day? What would you think about as you dozed off in bed?

You are a priest.

Your mental picture of a priest might cause you to resist the title. I don't mean the guy with the long robe and the collar who is always nice to the cashier. I am not referring to the overweight preacher with a short tie that talks in a deep voice and whose wife can play the piano. While there is nothing wrong with short ties and collars, they don't make you a priest.

You are a priest because God calls you a priest. You are a priest because God has made you one. God was speaking through Peter when he wrote, "You are a . . . royal priesthood" (1 Pet. 2:9).

Peter was not writing to a commune of priests. He was not writing to a Bible college filled with kids who were not allowed to download music or engage in coed swimming. He was not addressing a church staff or a ministerial association. Nor was he writing a seminary filled with future ministers and pastors.

Peter was writing to everyday normal people who were Christians. People like you. People with jobs, families, frustrations, worries, and daily pressure. He was talking to people who were wrestling with how their new faith would be lived out in a world with which they no longer fully identified. Through Peter, God told these people that they were priests. In the same way, God calls you a priest.

Your identity as a priest is a greater identity than you may realize.

People are often in search of a greater identity. They are dissatisfied with who they are. They dream of being someone else. They believe that a greater identity will allow them to do things they presently cannot do. A greater identity will enable them to go places they only dream of going and meet people they only fantasize about meeting.

Searching for a Greater Identity

Evidently Brian Jackson wanted a more prestigious identity. Evidently Brian Jackson was not fulfilled in his own skin. He wanted to be someone else.

Brian Jackson grew up in Pittsburgh, Pennsylvania, where the Steelers are everything to the people. The players are gods. The team is worshipped. Black and gold are everywhere. Kids grow up dreaming of being a Steeler. They dream of going where the Steelers go and meeting who the Steelers meet.

Brian Jackson's childhood dream was trapped in his adult body. Brian Jackson still longed for the identity of a Steeler. So Brian became a Steeler.

Brian studied the players whom he sought to emulate. He knew where they were born, where they went to school, what they drove, and the names of parents, kids, wives, and pets. He could recount with detail all the games "he" played.

We all know fans that are a bit obsessive, but Brian took his obsession to another level. He pretended to be the players.

To one girl he was Jerame Tuman, the Steeler's tight end. He showed her the cell numbers of fellow teammates and his "boyz" Hines Ward, Jerome Bettis, and Ike Taylor. He sped through town with her in his "ride" running red lights.

No one is gonna arrest me, I am a Steeler.

To another girl he was quarterback Ben Roethelisberger. He signed jerseys for her and her neighbors. He told her about his dog Zeus. He talked nonstop about himself as Roethelisberger, recounting details from recent trips.

To yet another girl he was Brian St. Pierre. He told her inside stories about his teammates. He signed footballs for her and kids in her neighborhood.

Brian Jackson *was* these players.

Each time he drove down the road wearing official football gloves, he became someone else. Each time he drove through the city bumping his music, he was another man. In his own mind he became a part of the team. He convinced himself that he and fellow teammate Hines were tight. He was in. The other players were his buddies.

He could go where a Steeler could go. He could meet girls like a Steeler.

However, Brian Jackson was discovered. Busted. Shown to be a fake. The girls learned of his scheme when they saw pictures of the real players in the papers or on TV. Brian faced felony charges for identity theft.

He longed for the identity of the players. He wanted to be someone else, someone who mattered. Brian pursued the benefits that came with being a Steeler. He wanted a greater identity than being Brian Jackson offered him. Jackson rambled as he admitted:

> I just idolize these guys and what they do, and
> the attention they get from women, and I just want
> that for myself, and I don't think I can do that on
> my own, and I just want to be them.[1]

Brian Jackson was so desperate for a greater identity that he was willing to steal it.

Do you ever find yourself searching for a greater identity?

I do.

And when I do, it is because I have forgotten my great identity as a priest of God. We cannot steal, buy, or earn our identity as priests. God has graciously given us this exciting identity. Our identity as a priest enables us to go where others have longed to go and meet who others have dreamed of meeting.

So what is the big deal about being a priest?

Where You Can Go

I am a huge basketball fan. My favorite T-shirt in college read, "Jesus is life. The rest is just basketball." Living in Miami for the Miami Heat's championship season in 2005–2006 was serious fun. For those of you who prefer watching Lifetime movies over ESPN's Sports Center, the Heat are a professional basketball team in Miami, Florida.

One day a business guy in our church gave me three Heat tickets. These tickets were phenomenal seats in the lower part of the arena. I brought two guys from our staff with me. We were enjoying the game when something amazing happened.

Someone from the Heat organization came to our seats and asked if we wanted to tour the locker room during the game. The locker room! The Heat official must have thought we were businessmen with some connections or potential long-term customers. We tried to act like we were expecting the invitation. We did not tell him we were pastors.

As we followed the Heat official through layers of security, we tried to contain our excitement. We attempted to act like the journey was no big deal, like we had done this kind of thing before. But while he was walking in front of us, we would turn to one another with one of those "I can't believe this" looks.

The Heat official took us to a corridor where the owner's son met us to give us the grand tour. The son of the owner of the Miami Heat took us through the final layer of security. We went to the weight room, the trainer's room, the player's lounge, and a practice gym. These were very cool places to be, but we wanted to get closer. We were eager to see the locker room. We wanted to go behind the scenes, behind the curtain where few people enter.

If you have ever played sports, you know the locker room is a special place. In the locker room the players gather before the game. The coach lays out the strategy. The team captain speaks up and challenges the players. The team unites and gets fired up for battle.

And we were invited to enter this special place. We saw Dwayne Wade's locker. We held one of Shaq's shoes. We saw Zo's gear. We stood in the center of the room where Coach Riley stands when he talks to his team. We smelled the magic of the room.

Or maybe that was something else.

Regardless, the moment was very special. We went back to our seats. And at the end of the night, we went back to our homes. When we told people where we had gone, you could see the envy in their eyes.

You went inside the Heat locker room during the game!

As a priest, you have the privilege to enter a much more special place than a smelly locker room. You are invited inside the most sacred place . . . the Most Holy Place.

INSIDE THE SPECIAL PLACE

The phrase "you are a royal priesthood" is a weighty phrase. Readers in the first century understood the fullness of this one statement. They grew up knowing about the privilege of being a priest in the Jewish culture. Just as Brian Jackson fantasized about being a Steeler, many boys grew up dreaming of being the high priest.

Part of the privilege was *where* the priest was able to go. The high priest held the privilege of entering the most sacred place in the Jewish culture. The high priest was able to go into what was called the Most Holy Place. Every God worshipper wanted to go there. Most people had read descriptions, but they could only imagine what it was really like. They heard stories, but only a select few ever saw the sacred place.

The Most Holy Place was the most important room in the temple and in the tabernacle before the temple was built. Only the high priest could go there. No one else held such an honor. No one else had the privilege. No one else was invited.

Now the first covenant had regulations for worship and also an earthly sanctuary. A tabernacle was set up. In its first room were the lampstand, the table and the consecrated bread; this was called the Holy Place. Behind the second curtain was a room called the Most Holy Place, which had the golden altar of incense and the gold-covered ark of the covenant. This ark contained the gold jar of manna, Aaron's staff that had budded, and the stone tablets of the covenant. Above the ark

were the cherubim of the Glory, overshadowing the atonement cover [mercy seat]. But we cannot discuss these things in detail now. When everything had been arranged like this, the priests entered regularly into the outer room to carry on their ministry. *But only the high priest entered the inner room,* and that only once a year, and never without blood, which he offered for himself and for the sins the people had committed in ignorance.
(Heb. 9:1–7 NIV, emphasis added)

Both the temple and the tabernacle were divided into three main parts: the outer court, the Holy Place (the first room), and the Most Holy Place (the inner room). Surrounding the temple's outer court was the court of the Gentiles. The court of the Gentiles was intended to give Gentiles (non-Jewish people) a place to worship God. But the court was far removed from the Most Holy Place.

The outer court was the biggest part of the temple. The outer court was where Jewish people could worship. In the outer court there was the bronze altar where sacrifices were made and the bronze basin where priests washed their bloody hands.

Then there was the Holy Place. The Holy Place is where the priests could enter. While the Holy Place was more sacred and special than the outer court, it still was not the best.

The place where everyone longed to be was behind the second curtain. Behind the veil was the Most Holy Place. In the Most Holy Place was the ark of covenant. The lid of the ark was called the mercy seat. The mercy seat was where God and man met. When God first gave instructions regarding the mercy seat, He said:

> "Set the mercy seat on top of the ark and put the testimony that I will give you into the ark. I will meet with you there above the mercy seat, between the two cherubim that are over the ark of the testimony; I will speak with you from there about all that I command you regarding the Israelites." (Exod. 25:21–22)

God met with man in the Most Holy Place. Above the mercy seat.

BACK IN TIME

Let's go back in time. Back before Christ came. Back to the days of the tabernacle and temple. . . .

We are watching from outside the temple area because we are only allowed in the court of the Gentiles. We worship God from afar. We see the activity in the outer court, and we wish we could get closer. But the court of the Gentiles is the only place we can gather. Unless you are a Jew, you are stuck in the court of the Gentiles, way outside the action.

It is not even the nosebleed section.

In archaeological digs of Herod's temple, signs were uncovered warning Gentiles (people like me) not to come any closer. One sign read: "No foreigner is to enter within the enclosure around the temple area. Whoever is caught will have himself to blame for his death which will follow."[2]

Ouch. So unless you are a Jew, you should stay out here with me.

We notice the priests who are able to go further than the outer court. We envy them as they go behind the first veil into the Holy Place. We wonder what they are experiencing, what they are sensing. They are fairly close to the Most Holy Place. And fairly close to the mercy seat. We know that at the mercy seat, God will meet with man!

We look for the high priest.

We want to see the one guy who holds the honor to go behind the second curtain. We wonder what he is thinking. No doubt <u>he is fearful.</u> He will meet with a holy and righteous God. No doubt he is grateful. He gets to enter the presence of God.

We wonder what it would be like to have that privilege, to be the one who is able to enter the Most Holy Place. We wonder what it would be like to go where he goes. To meet who he meets.

We whisper that if we would have that honor, we would never take it for granted. We would be so grateful. If we had that opportunity, we would savor the time with God. We would not squander the moment. We would enjoy the presence of our God.

BACK TO NOW

With that history in mind, Peter says that you are a royal priest. You have the privilege to enter the Most Holy Place. The writer of Hebrews reminds us of the honor we hold as priests of God:

> Therefore, brothers, since we have *confidence*
> to enter the Most Holy Place by the blood of Jesus,
> by a new and living way opened for us through
> the curtain, that is, his body, and since we have

a great priest over the house of God, let us draw
near to God with a sincere heart in full assurance
of faith, having our hearts sprinkled to cleanse
us from a guilty conscience and having our bodies washed with pure water. (Heb. 10:19–22 NIV,
emphasis added)

Amazingly, you can walk past the court of the Gentiles,
through the outer court, and into the Holy Place. And you
don't have to stop there. You can enter the Most Holy Place.

Confidently. Not with fear, worry, insecurity, or doubt.
But with confidence. You are a priest, and you do not need
to tiptoe into the presence of God.

Confidence is different from cockiness.

While you would be foolish to come before God with
cockiness, you can approach Him with confidence. You are
welcome in the presence of God.

This was huge news to the readers in the first century.
The concept of the Most Holy Place was way out of their
league. Entering the Most Holy Place was not something
they associated with confidence. The thought of entering the
presence of God was frightening. They heard stories about
people who had tried to enter the temple.

They heard the story of King Uzziah. . . .

Where Kings Can't Go

Uzziah was a Jewish king who lived during the temple
system before Jesus came. Uzziah was a successful and God-
fearing man. As long as he sought the Lord, God gave him
success (see 2 Chron. 26:1–5).

He amassed land. He built towns and towers. He had a well-trained army. The kingdom was growing. His fame spread far and wide (see 2 Chron. 26:6–15). The blogs about him were positive. The polls indicated that a high percentage of people believed in his leadership.

The shareholders were excited. The board of directors was thrilled with the results. Investors were lining up to finance Uzziah's next building campaign. He was well-respected and well-known. Families named their kids after him.

God was showing favor. Uzziah would be known as a great king, as a man who feared God, a man whom God chose to bless. Unfortunately his story has a different ending. . . .

After Uzziah became powerful, his pride led to his downfall. He was unfaithful to the LORD his God, and entered the temple of the LORD to burn incense on the altar of incense. Azariah the priest with eighty other courageous priests of the LORD followed him in. They confronted him and said, "It is not right for you, Uzziah, to burn incense to the LORD. That is for the priests, the descendants of Aaron, who have been consecrated to burn incense. Leave the sanctuary, for you have been unfaithful; and you will not be honored by the LORD God." Uzziah, who had a censer in his hand ready to burn incense, became angry. While he was raging at the priests in their presence before the incense altar in the LORD's temple, leprosy broke out on his forehead. When Azariah the chief priest and all the other priests looked at him, they saw that he had leprosy on his forehead, so they hurried him out. Indeed, he himself was eager to leave, because the LORD had afflicted him. King Uzziah had leprosy until the day he died. He lived in a separate house—leprous, and excluded from the temple of the LORD. Jotham his son had charge of the palace and governed the people of the land. The other events of Uzziah's reign, from beginning to end, are recorded by the prophet Isaiah son of Amoz. Uzziah rested with his fathers and was buried near them in a field for burial that belonged to the kings, for people said, "He had leprosy." (2 Chron. 26:16–23 NIV)

Uzziah ended his life with his legacy simply being "he had leprosy." For a Jewish man to have leprosy meant that he was cut off from everyone. He lived in isolation. And because the Jewish people associated sickness with sin, his leprosy was a constant reminder of his downfall to himself and the people.

He was buried in a field that belonged to the kings, but he was not buried in the royal tombs that were set apart for the political leaders. Even in his death, he was quarantined from the success he once enjoyed.

All that was said of Uzziah was, "He had leprosy."

Perhaps school classes went on field trips to the royal tombs, and they would see his grave nearby in a field. The teacher would point to the grave and say, "There is Uzziah. He had leprosy."

Perhaps when the family reunion happened once every few years, a nephew would ask about Uncle Uzzie. And someone would say, "Oh, he had leprosy."

What went wrong in Uzziah's story?

Uzziah barged into the Holy Place in the temple. God reserved the Holy Place for priests. Only priests who were descendents of Aaron were allowed to approach the altar of incense (Num. 16:40). Evidently Uzziah believed he was above this command. After all, he was the king. He felt he deserved to go where he wanted, when he wanted.

He learned that there are some places where kings cannot go.

Even successful ones.

Eighty priests went in after Uzziah. As priests, they belonged in the Holy Place. They told Uzziah he was in the wrong place. He shrugged off the rebuke. And God struck him with leprosy. He was plagued with leprosy until the day he died.

Uzziah was a famous and effective king. Yet he was not allowed inside the temple. His wealth, success, status, crown, and skill were insufficient to gain him access to the presence of God.

Uzziah was not qualified to enter the Holy Place. Much less the Most Holy Place.

If you are a follower of Christ, God has qualified you to enter His presence. You are invited because you are His priest. You can go further than Uzziah. You are able to go where a king could not.

You have *confidence* to enter the Most Holy Place.

WHAT CHANGED?

Why can you enter the presence of God when people like Uzziah could not? What gives you the honor of entering the Most Holy Place? What is different now from the centuries of life under the temple system?

Christ changed everything.

Christ has given you access into the presence of God. He has made it possible for you to enter the Most Holy Place. Let's go back to Hebrews 10:

> Therefore, brothers, since we have confidence to enter the Most Holy Place *by the blood of Jesus*, by a new and living way opened for us through the curtain, that is, his body, and since we have a great priest over the house of God, let us draw near to God. (Heb. 10:19–22 NIV, emphasis added)

During the days of the tabernacle and the temple, the high priest would sacrifice an animal on the bronze altar in the outer court. The high priest would do this one day a year called Yom Kippur, or the Day of Atonement. The blood sacrifice was to cover the sins committed by the people in ignorance (Heb. 9:7). Regular sacrifices were made to cover the sins that people knew they committed. But once a year a sacrifice was made for the sins the people did not realize they committed.

The high priest would take blood from the sacrifice with him into the Most Holy Place. He would sprinkle the blood on the mercy seat. He could not enter the presence of God without blood from the sacrifice.

Christ changed everything. He came to this earth two thousand years ago and willingly laid down His life (John 10:18). He sacrificed Himself so that we could gain access to God. He placed Himself on the cross, the sacrificial altar.

It is no coincidence that God sent His Son to die during a time in history when death by crucifixion was the norm.

The death had to be bloody because "without the shedding of blood there is no forgiveness" of sins (Heb. 9:22). So at just the right time, Christ came to this earth (Rom. 5:6). Christ's sacrifice was once and for all because He offered His own blood (Heb. 9:24–28).

It is also no coincidence that Jesus was crucified during the Jewish Passover celebration, when lambs were being sacrificed. Jesus is "the Lamb of God, who takes away the sin of the world" (John 1:29). His death had to be bloody so you could enter the Most Holy Place—so you could enter the presence of God.

When my friends and I were invited to tour the inner rooms of the Miami Heat facility, it was because the owner's son was with us. We would not have been allowed behind the layers of security without him. We were able to enjoy a few moments in the locker room because of the owner's son. You are invited into the presence of God by the blood of God's Son. Without the Son, you would be far removed from the Most Holy Place.

In the temple and tabernacle system, a curtain separated the Most Holy Place from the rest of the temple. From the rest of the world.

From you.

This curtain separated us from God. We could not peer behind the curtain. We could not go behind the veil. The curtain was a constant reminder that the presence of God was inaccessible.

But when Christ died, a new and living way opened for us. As He was breathing His last breath on the cross, a miraculous event occurred. . . .

> And when Jesus had cried out again in a loud voice, he gave up his spirit. At that moment the curtain of the temple was torn in two from top to bottom. The earth shook and the rocks split. (Matt. 27:50–51 NIV)

As Christ's body was torn, the curtain in the temple was torn. *Because* Christ's body was torn, the veil was torn. The Most Holy Place became accessible. Christ changed everything.

OK, WHERE?

So Christ has made me a priest. And I can enter the Most Holy Place.

But where is it? Where is this special place? Do I need to travel to some remote location? Is there a secret room at the church that I have not heard about? Do I purchase my own portable Most Holy Place at some Christian outlet mall in Texas?

There is no room. There is no curtain.

God no longer meets with man in an earthly Most Holy Place. His throne is not in a temple, church, or room. His throne is in heaven.

> Now the main point of what is being said is this: we have this kind of high priest, who sat down at the right hand of the throne of the Majesty in the heavens, a minister of the sanctuary and the true tabernacle, which the Lord set up, and not man. For every high priest is appointed to offer gifts and sacrifices; therefore it was necessary for this priest also to have something to offer. Now if

He were on earth, He wouldn't be a priest, since
there are those offering the gifts prescribed by the
law. These serve as a copy and shadow of the heavenly things, as Moses was warned when he was
about to complete the tabernacle. For He said, "Be
careful that you make everything according to the
pattern that was shown to you on the mountain."
(Heb. 8:1–5)

The earthly tabernacle and temple were only photo-
copies of the real thing. The real and true temple is in
heaven. The original mercy seat is the throne of God.

Now we are able to go directly to the throne of God to
find grace and mercy. We don't physically go to the throne
of God, but spiritually we do. We don't meet with God
in a building somewhere. We are able to meet with Him
anywhere; therefore, you can enter the presence of God
wherever you are.

I always get uncomfortable when I hear people talk about
a church building as God's house as if He lives there. As if
God wakes up early, makes coffee, and anticipates my arrival
at a worship service or mass. As if He turns out the lights
when I leave and hopes I come back next week to visit Him.

Lots of church people actually believe God lives in the
church. They would not say so directly, but they reveal their
belief through other statements and actions. Let me share
some examples. . . .

While serving as a youth pastor, a few parents were
upset because we used "rock" music in our student worship
services. The music was filled with lyrics that were written
to God, but the parents thought the music was "not the type
of music that should be played in God's house."

But when I would visit their homes or ride in their vehicles, the music they played was not the kind of music they advocated we play in worship services. It was not even what would be called "Christian music." They held a different set of standards for the music they would listen to throughout the week than they did for the music that was "appropriate for church."

In my twenties I thought this was hypocritical.

Now I think it is bad theology. His ears are not more sensitive in the church building because He does not live in the church. He does not have a different set of values in a home or car than He does in a church.

And why don't we tell people to dress up more to go to "the house of God"?

Well, because we are not going to the house of God. We are not dressing up to go impress God at His home. God does not live there.

God lives in a mobile home. He lives within you, wherever you go.

We are the house of God. He lives within us who are Christians; therefore, we can meet with Him anywhere.

The problem with viewing a building as God's house is that if we are not careful, we live as different people everywhere else. We become inconsistent in our faith. Because we tend to meet with God only in the places we view as sacred, we must have an accurate view of where God lives. Viewing the church building as a more sacred place than other environments in our lives insults the omnipresence of God, the sacrifice of Christ, and the privilege we have as royal priests.

Spiritually you can go to the throne of God. Right where you are. You are invited. Right now.

RIGHT NOW?

Right now you can meet with God. In fact, you have an even greater privilege than the high priest.

The high priest could only go into the Most Holy Place one day each year on the Day of Atonement. The high priests and all of the Jewish people looked forward to this day. Their spiritual slate would be symbolically wiped clean. Their sins would be covered.

On the Day of Atonement the temple would be filled early in the morning as the people were eager with anticipation. The high priest would spend the morning going through many rituals and sacrifices preparing for the moment when he would enter the Most Holy Place. He would sacrifice animals on the bronze altar in the outer court. After cleansing himself, he would go behind the veil and be with God in the Most Holy Place. But he did not stay long. "He hurried out, and the people breathed a sigh of relief at seeing him. Had he entered the Most Holy Place ceremonially unclean, he would have been struck dead."[3]

You don't have to wait for a special day. And you don't need to rush. You can spend time with God right now.

You may enter the Most Holy Place. Anytime. Anywhere. And you may meet with God.

What would tomorrow be like if you remembered that you are a priest? What would be different in the morning? How would the drive to work or throughout town change? How would you approach the day? What would you think about as you dozed off in bed?

What should be different? How should you respond to this reality?

Slow Down

Slow down. Take time to enter the presence of God.

Psalm 46:10 says, "Be still, and know that I am God" (NIV). The command for us is to be still. Whether we are still or not, God is still God. But our stillness is closely connected with our realization that He is God.

When we are still, we are reminded of His greatness. When we slow down, we are more able to listen. If we are never still, we miss what He is doing. We miss His invitation to enter His presence. We miss His invitation because we are always on the go, always in a rush.

The Washington Post recently conducted an interesting research experiment. They hired one of the world's best violinists to play at a busy metro stop. His name is Joshua Bell. He typically plays in major concert halls for sold-out audiences. People pay hundreds of dollars to watch him play the violin. He plays a *Gibson ex Huberman* hand-crafted in 1713 by Antonio Stradivari. Reportedly, Bell paid 3.5 million dollars for the violin.

In other words, the dude is really good.

On Friday morning, January 12, 2007, Joshua Bell arrived at the DC metro stop. Three days before his metro stop concert, he filled Boston's Symphony Hall. On this morning he pulled the multimillion-dollar violin out of the case and placed the case on the floor. He stood behind it. He seeded his case with a couple of bucks. And began to play.

During rush hour.

This world-renowned and highly regarded musician played for people at the metro stop. The guy whose name and skill demands huge ticket prices played for free. People usually watch him from afar. He is usually on a stage in a large concert hall. Now his listeners could stand a few feet from him. He played six classical pieces for forty-three consecutive minutes.

What happened? How did people respond?

People rushed by.

Seven people stopped to listen; 1,097 people passed by Bell during his concert. Most people did not even slow down. They were too busy, too preoccupied with the tasks of their day. Some placed dimes or quarters in his case. He continued to play as people marched past him. People missed the opportunity to listen to the music of one of the world's most talented musicians.

Except for one lady.

Stacy Furukawa stood in awe and listened. She previously watched Bell perform at a concert, a concert at the Library of Congress. She was shocked that people were placing change in his case. She could not believe that people were not taking advantage of the front row seats.

Stacy stood by and admired. She listened intently. The busyness and business of the day could wait. She had to slow down. She had to take advantage of the moment. She commented to *The Washington Post*:

> "It was the most astonishing thing I've ever
> seen in Washington," Furukawa says. "Joshua Bell
> was standing there playing at rush hour, and people
> were not stopping, and not even looking, and some
> were flipping quarters at him! Quarters! I wouldn't
> do that to anybody. I was thinking, *Omigosh, what
> kind of a city do I live in that this could happen?*"[4]

Would I have stopped? Would I have slowed down and savored the moment? Would you have slowed your pace? What was the difference between Stacy and everyone else? She recognized him.

She knew his musical voice. His music was familiar to her. To everyone else, the music was just another sound in an iPod world filled with nonstop noise. To Stacy the sound was meaningful, beautiful, and important.

Jesus said that His sheep listen to His voice (John 10:27). His sheep listen to His voice because they know Him. They know His voice.

How amazing is God's voice to you? How beautiful is the music He plays for you? Will you stop to listen to Him? Will you slow down?

Stay Connected

The Miami Heat spanked the Dallas Mavericks to win the NBA title in 2006. A buddy with season tickets took me to game 4 of the NBA Finals in Miami. The seats were good, but we brought binoculars so we could get some up-close looks of Mark Cuban (Dallas Owner) complaining to the refs. And Cuban graciously obliged.

During the game I was looking through the binoculars, and I noticed a guy from our church with floor seats. Feet on the floor at the NBA Finals! I could not believe it. I was a bit jealous. But in a godly sort of way.

A few days later I saw my friend with floor seats at our Saturday night service. I approached him about how he scored such great seats. We laughed that I was spying on him with binoculars.

Game 5 was on Sunday night. Kaye and I watched it from home, on our 19-inch television from our college days. I thought how sweet it would be to be at the game.

Monday morning I checked my e-mail at the office. Uncontrollably a loud scream erupted from my mouth. My floor seat friend had e-mailed me on Sunday, asking if I would like to go with him to the Heat game. But I did not check my e-mail until Monday morning.

I missed it!

I missed the phenomenal privilege of floor seats for the NBA Finals. I was invited, but I missed the opportunity. While this story is painfully tragic to hoop fans, it is not nearly as tragic as our missed opportunities with God.

We are continually invited into the Most Holy Place. We are invited to the best seat in the world. We are invited to enjoy the presence of God, to be with Him, to be before Him. But we often miss the opportunity.

Why do we miss the ongoing opportunity to enjoy the presence of God?

Sadly we often treat prayer as this thing we do at important junctures in our day instead of continual communication with God. We pray in the morning. We pray before meals. We pray at bedtime. And if we are really good Christians, we pray before important meetings.

But what about the rest of the day? The rest of our lives?

When we view prayer as something we only do at scheduled moments in our day, we miss the opportunity to be continually in the presence of God. Perhaps Paul was reflecting on this truth when he wrote, "Pray constantly" (1 Thess. 5:17).

Pray constantly. Stay connected.

Spiritual BlackBerry

So that we can always be connected, our culture provides BlackBerry devices. If you think a BlackBerry is only a small berry you picked as a kid, it's time you got out more. Maybe you can use your dial-up Internet to do a Web search.

A BlackBerry is a phone, e-mail device, Web browser, and organizer rolled into one small personal handheld device. A BlackBerry allows you instantly to receive e-mails from people. If you have a BlackBerry, you are always connected. Many people insist they need these devices. They always want to be tapped into the world around them. They do not want to miss an opportunity.

If I had owned a BlackBerry during the Heat championship run, I would not have missed the game. I would have received the e-mail as it was sent. But because I only checked e-mails at important junctures in my day, I missed the invitation. I missed the opportunity because I was not always connected.

What if we were as desperate to stay connected to God as we are to other people in our lives? What if we lived with a spiritual BlackBerry?

What if we made our vehicles mobile versions of the Most Holy Place so we could drive in the presence of God? What would that look like in your life?

What if we made our beds the Most Holy Place, and we snoozed off to sleep each night in the presence of God? What would you think about as you dozed off?

What would change if we made our offices and our workplaces the Most Holy Place and we invited the presence of God into these environments? How would you approach the day differently?

Let me be transparent. Sadly, the missed invitation into the Most Holy Place does not seem to bother me as much as the missed invitation to a ball game. Why doesn't my neglect of the presence of God bother me as much as missing a hoops game? Why don't I yell out a scream of regret each time I neglect the presence of God?

What about you?

The reality: You are a royal priest. You can enter the presence of God. You can meet with Him. Anytime. Anywhere.

The response: Slow down. Stay connected. Keep your spiritual BlackBerry on.

Group Discussion Questions

1. What do you think King Uzziah (and others like him) would say to us today about our privilege to go to the Most Holy Place? *don't understand.*

2. Why do you think people tend to view the church building as more sacred than other locations? Why is this unhealthy? *It gives a false example of what we w/ Christ should be. Everyone dresses up, doesn't make bad jokes, and talks abt God.*

3. Read Hebrews 10:19–22 together as a group. What is the most meaningful part of this passage to you? Why? *lot of emotion 21-22, We can draw new in ABS*

4. How does an understanding of the tabernacle and temple system impact your view of Christ's sacrifice? *Makes me appreciate my easy access to God + reminded of his holiness.*

5. Read 1 Thessalonians 5:17 as a group. Is this
    realistic? What would this look like in everyday
    life? *Yes, just thinking prayer. You don't have to get on your knees everytime you pray*

6. What is one area of your life that you can make
    "the Most Holy Place"? *Right before bed.*

7. How can we fight the busyness in our lives so we
    can slow down and listen to God's voice?

    — set aside time
    — Filling of HS

CHAPTER 4
||||||||||||||||||||||||

You Are the Bride
(holy)

*As God made man in His own image, so He
made earthly marriage in the image of His
own eternal marriage with His people.*

—GEOFFREY BROMILEY

In the early 1970s, a social scientist named Philip Zimbardo led a team of scientists from Stanford University in an interesting experiment. The team built a mock prison in the basement of the University's psychology department. The scientists placed advertisements in the local papers looking for volunteers who would participate in the experiment. Zimbardo and his colleagues selected twenty-four people to participate, choosing the ones who appeared to be the most emotionally stable and healthy.

Half of the group was randomly selected to be prison guards. They were given military-style guard uniforms and dark glasses. They were told their responsibility was to keep order.

The other half of the group became the prisoners. They were arrested in their homes, cuffed, brought to a real police station, fingerprinted, and then blindfolded for the trip to the mock prison. They wore prison clothes with numbers on the front and back of the clothing.

The number became their identity.

They were only allowed to refer to themselves and others by their numbers. In post interviews with the prisoners in the experiment, they confessed that when their identity became a number, they felt helpless and hopeless. Four of the prisoners were pulled from the experiment early because of emotional breakdowns including extreme depression, crying, rage, and anxiety. Other prisoners incited rebellions and riots against the guards.

When the mock prisoners forgot who they really were, they became depressed. Their self-perception impacted their thinking, attitude, and ultimately their behavior. When they believed that they were criminals, they began to live like criminals.

The experiment was intended to last two weeks, but Zimbardo shut it down after six days because of the chaos that was ensuing. When he was dismissing some of the mock prisoners, he needed to remind them that they were not prisoners, that the scenario was not real.[1]

Spiritual Mock Prison

Unfortunately for many people, life seems like a long and painful prison experiment. Though Christ has set believers free from the prison of sin, many Christians live as if they are in bondage to guilt. Many Christians live defeated because they believe the lie that they are prisoners of sin.

The reality is that Christ has set us free from sin.

In fact, the word *sinner* is never used in the Bible of a Christian.[2] While we still sin, and will struggle with sin, our identity is no longer that of a sinner. We are brand-new people.

Just as the guards in the prison experiment bombarded the mock prisoners with messages about their identity, there is an accuser who constantly bombards you with messages. Satan is the accuser. In fact, Satan's name literally means accuser. And day and night he hurls accusations about you (Rev. 12:10). He knows that if he can cause you to believe you are a prisoner of sin, you will live that way.

You have heard the accusations. . . .

- There is no way God could forgive you for what you have done.
- Your past is so dark that God will not use you.
- Other Christians never struggle like you do.
- Look at the mess you have created. There is no way God can love you.
- God is ashamed of people like you.

While the enemy hurls inaccurate insults your way, God reminds you of the truth of your new identity in His Word. The accuser tells you that you are guilty; God says that there is no condemnation for those who are in Christ (Rom. 8:1). The enemy says you are nothing more than a sinner; Christ declares you are no longer a slave to sin (Rom. 6:6).

While the accuser tells you that you are filthy and unclean, God says you have received His righteousness (1 Cor. 1:30). The accuser points to prison walls; God says you have been set free (Gal. 5:1). The accuser points to all your previous sin; God declares you righteous in Christ (2 Cor. 5:21).

You have been set free from spiritual prison; so don't live as if you are a prisoner.

Please do not misread me. I am not suggesting that thinking you are free makes you free. If you are not spiritually free, no amount of thinking will alter the reality that you are a slave to sin, in spiritual bondage. If you are still in spiritual bondage, your heart needs to be transformed, not your thinking.

However, I am suggesting that you remember the reality of who you are, that you understand what God declares to be true about you. You are not thinking yourself into a state of being forgiven, as if your thoughts changed reality. You are not telling yourself you are free to cope with the spiritual prison. You *actually are* forgiven and free.

Zimbardo was compelled to tell the mock prisoners that the prison was not real. The nightmare was an experiment. God is compelled to tell you the same thing; the prison is not real. You are free. You are forgiven.

To drive home the point, God calls you His bride.

The Bride

Unless you have dozed off at every wedding you attended, you have heard the famous passage about God making two people one. When God first set the foundation for marriage in the book of Genesis, He said that *two people will become one flesh* (Gen. 2:24).

God is describing the depth of a relationship where a man and woman become completely united physically, emotionally, and spiritually. He is describing a relationship where they can finish each other's sentences and know each other fully. For God, marriage unites two people completely. They become one.

Earthly marriage is a reflection of our eternal relationship with God. Just as God made man in His own image, God created marriage in the image of His relationship to us. The apostle Paul compares our relationship with God to marriage:

> Husbands, love your wives, just as Christ loved the church and gave himself up for her to make her holy, cleansing her by the washing with water through the word, and to present her to himself as a radiant church, without stain or wrinkle or any other blemish, but holy and blameless. In this same way, husbands ought to love their wives as their own bodies. He who loves his wife loves himself. After all, no one ever hated his own body, but he feeds and cares for it, just as Christ does the church—for we are members of his body. "For this reason a man will leave his father and mother and be united to his wife, and the two will become one flesh. This is a profound mystery—but I am talking about Christ and the church." (Eph. 5:25–32 NIV)

The *profound mystery* of the passage is that you are now the body and bride of Christ. When you became a

Glitch: We are not equal to God as in marriage.

Christian, you were united with Christ. You are one with Him. He cares for you as He cares for His own body because you are His body. And His bride.

Whose Am I?

"Who am I?" is the question we are unpacking throughout this book. However, we typically answer that question with another question: "Whose am I?"

Think back to your middle school years. So much of your day depended on your relationships. You worried about whom you would sit by on the bus because, in your mind, that indicated who you were as a person. Or you cared greatly about where you would sit during lunch. Or whose locker you would stand by during recess. The relationships were critical because your relationships defined you as a person.

Has much really changed since middle school? We still interpret our identity by our relationships. The context is different, but the reality is the same.

Who wants to hire me? Who in the office wants to have lunch with me? Who do I belong to? To whom do I matter? Who cares for me? Who thinks of me at night? Who wants to have me on their team?

Much of our identity is wrapped up in our relationships. Our relationships and our identity are inseparable. No wonder rejection is so painful. Our identity is threatened. We fear maybe we are not who we thought we were.

Whose are you?

Jesus declares you are His bride. He chose the highest expression of commitment between two people to express

His commitment to you. Your identity is wrapped up in the reality of your relationship with Christ.

And because you are His, you are completely forgiven.

COMPLETELY FORGIVEN

As I type this on my laptop, I am on my back porch, and the morning sun is beginning to shine brightly. And I am very frustrated.

When I began writing outside this morning, the sky was still dark. But as light entered the day, the sun exposed smudges on my laptop screen. And as the sun rose, the smudges became more and more noticeable. The bright light exposed the blemishes.

I hate the smudges. I want the screen to be clean.

I attempted to use my T-shirt to clean the screen, but my attempt made the screen look worse. I retrieved some napkins, hoping they would erase the blemishes. Same result. My second attempt created more smudges. Frustrated, I hastily ran to the kitchen and grabbed Windex from under the sink.

Surely Windex will clean my screen.

But my uncertain hands failed. And evidently Windex is not the best solution for a smudgy screen. All my attempts fell short. In fact, they made the screen look worse and only revealed how insufficient I am to wipe the screen clean.

In the quiet of the morning, God used my inability to clean a screen to remind me of my inability to erase my own sin.

God is light, and He exposes the sin in our lives. When we press toward God, we realize how blemished and stained we are. We frantically attempt to erase our own sin, but our attempts only reveal how incapable we are. Ultimately our sin offends God; therefore, He is the one who must wipe the slate clean. And He is the only one able to wipe the slate clean.

As His bride, you are completely forgiven by Him because His death cleansed you wholly. He erased every spot and blemish. In fact, look how God describes and illustrates His forgiveness of your sins. . . .

- *As far as the east is from the west, so far has He removed our transgressions from us* (Ps. 103:12).
- *You will cast all our sins into the depths of the sea* (Mic. 7:19).
- *You have thrown all my sins behind Your back* (Isa. 38:17).
- *I will forgive their wrongdoing and never again remember their sin* (Jer. 31:34).
- *Though your sins are like scarlet, they will be white as snow* (Isa. 1:18).

As the forgiven bride of Christ, you are wearing white.

WEARING WHITE

On November 9, 1996, I married Kaye Marie Kennedy. She became Kaye Geiger. We were married at the church where I was serving as youth pastor. I walked into the auditorium with my pastor and my father, who was my best man. I was a bit nervous. A lot of people were staring at me.

Then the music started. And Kaye began to walk down the aisle.

Toward me.

The church did not have a center aisle, so the standing guests blocked my view. Ignoring the instructions from my pastor, I walked over to the aisle Kaye was walking down. I had to see her. She was amazingly beautiful. She glowed. It was a holy moment.

I knew Kaye was a virgin. Several months before our wedding, Kaye gave me a letter she wrote to her future husband while she was in high school. She did not know me yet. The letter was written to whoever her spouse would be.

I was living like a fool in New Orleans. She was living pure in small town North Louisiana. Yet in high school she committed to be sexually pure. She committed to remain a virgin until her wedding night. And she wrote of her commitment in a letter to her future spouse.

The letter reads, "I do not know who you are or when we will meet. But I want you to know I love you now. I will be faithful to you now. I will keep myself sexually pure for you. You will be the only one to have all of me."

Back to the wedding . . . As Kaye marched toward me robed in white, the moment was holy and priceless. And not because of the cost of the dress. In fact, we borrowed the dress from her sister-in-law because we were broke. The moment was priceless because of the symbolic meaning of the white dress. Kaye was a pure bride.

As she walked down the aisle, I looked upon her with pride and admiration. I was so thankful to have her as mine. I was grateful to be united with her.

As His bride, you are wearing white.

"He has clothed me with the garments of salvation and wrapped me with a robe of righteousness" (Isa. 61:10). The Bible even describes a special ceremony in heaven called the wedding of the Lamb (Rev. 19:7 NIV) where you will be forever united with Christ.

As a dude, nothing excites me about wearing a white wedding dress. But I am thrilled that God has chosen to purify me, to forgive me of everything. The reality that God views me as holy and pure is amazing.

I do not deserve to wear white. I am not a spiritual virgin. I have messed up a ton. I still do. Yet Jesus looks at me as I looked at Kaye that day in November of '96.

He looks at you that way too. He has adorned you in a robe of righteousness. He sees you as His perfect bride, and He looks upon you with joy.

BUT HOW?

How am I His pure bride when I still sin?

Since you have been united with Christ, all of His righteousness and purity was credited to your account.

When Kaye and I married, we were united. From that moment all of "my" possessions became "our" possessions. No longer was there "my" stuff and "her" stuff, but everything became "our" stuff. All of my possessions became hers.

For Kaye our union was not a really big gain because I did not bring much to the table. I still drive the '95 Nissan truck I bought in college. Lucky her.

But Christ brings everything to the marriage. We bring nothing but our sin and shame, yet we receive His righteousness. Theologians speak of the "Great Exchange," which took place on the cross. Christ became sin by paying the penalty for our sin. In exchange He gave us His righteousness, His perfection.

You are the bride of Christ not because you have chosen to be a good person or to live well. You are the bride of Christ because Christ brought His righteousness into the relationship.

The thought of His righteousness being credited to my account reminds me of the first time I won a million dollars.

At least, I thought I won a million dollars. I was ten years old and home during summer break. I picked up the mail from the mailbox and thumbed through it. My mouth dropped as I beheld an envelope claiming my parents were millionaires.

The Publishers Clearing House envelope declared we were winners. At least the **BIG BOLD** print indicated we were. One million dollars would be credited to our account.

I could not believe it! I leaped through the house toward the phone. I called my dad to tell him the news. I did not understand why he was not more excited.

My dad was not excited because he knew better. He knew of the advertising ploy to attract subscriptions. He did not expect the prize patrol to be waiting for him when he came home from work. His years on Earth hardened him to the marketing campaigns and promises of free gifts to consumers. He knew one million dollars would not be automatically credited to his bank account. He knew the world does not operate in such a manner.

But Christ does.

Christ freely credits His righteousness to your eternal bank account. The moment you said "I do" to an eternal relationship with God, you became His bride and received

His righteousness. And His righteousness cancels all your sin.

A Crazy Story

The reality that Christians are the bride of Christ is illustrated in the Old Testament through the explicit story of Hosea and Gomer. Hosea was a prophet who ministered during a very rebellious period in Israel's history. God chose an interesting way to get the attention of His people.

> When the LORD began to speak through Hosea, the LORD said to him, "Go, take to yourself an adulterous wife and children of unfaithfulness, because the land is guilty of the vilest adultery in departing from the LORD." So he married Gomer daughter of Diblaim, and she conceived and bore him a son. (Hosea 1:2–3 NIV)

Yes, you read the verses correctly. God told Hosea to marry a prostitute. He did so with a purpose because the people in Israel were guilty of spiritual adultery. They were chasing other lovers, other gods (little "g"). They turned away from God and were worshipping idols.

So for one huge object lesson, God asks Hosea to marry a hooker.

Can you imagine Hosea bringing Gomer home to meet his parents? Meeting your future in-laws for the first time is stressful enough without having a prostitute fiancée.

Hosea marries Gomer despite his knowledge that she would be unfaithful. And as expected, Gomer is unfaithful to Hosea. The first child they have is Hosea's. We don't know if the other ones are his or not. Hosea probably did not know either.

Eventually she left him to pursue others.

Hosea was humiliated. His bride left him for others, and everyone knew it. People in town told jokes about Hosea. As he walked down the streets, he looked into the eyes of other men wondering if they were with his wife. He tucked his children into bed at night and wondered where his wife was sleeping.

Amazingly, Hosea does not wait for Gomer to return home. Instead he pursues her.

> The LORD said to me, "Go, show your love
> to your wife again, though she is loved by another
> and is an adulteress. Love her as the LORD loves
> the Israelites, though they turn to other gods and
> love the sacred raisin cakes." So I bought her for
> fifteen shekels of silver and about a homer and a
> lethek of barley. Then I told her, "You are to live
> with me many days; you must not be a prostitute or
> be intimate with any man, and I will live with you."
> (Hosea 3:1–3 NIV)

God told Hosea to find Gomer, to show love . . . again. God instructed Hosea to pursue Gomer to illustrate how God pursues His people, His bride. God does not wait in a rocking chair for us to come to Him. He is not a passive God. He actively seeks us.

Not only did Hosea pursue Gomer, but he also bought her.

Evidently Gomer's sinful life caught up with her. She was poor and destitute and selling herself into slavery. Hosea found her at the local slave auction. The normal price of a slave was thirty shekels. Hosea did not have thirty so he gave all his money and paid the balance with barley. Hosea, at a public slave auction, pays with all he has for his own wife.

God's love for us is like Hosea's love for Gomer. We were slaves to sin, and Christ was humiliated in order to buy us back. Publicly He was mocked and abused. He paid not with money or with barley but with His own life. To give you the identity of His bride, Christ purchased you.

Hosea told Gomer to forsake other lovers, to live with him. And as Hosea instructed Gomer to be faithful to him, God has instructed you to forsake others and to live out your identity as His bride.

So how should you live as His bride?

1. REMEMBER YOU ARE HIS BRIDE

As you live, remember you are the pure and forgiven bride of Christ. Remembering your identity as a pure bride should lead you to live pure and blameless. Purity is your new identity. To live impure is to not live the reality of who you really are. To live impure is to revert to your old identity.

As the bride you were given new clothes. You now wear white. Do not put on your old clothes. Live in the new clothes.

> You were taught with regards to your former
> way of life, to put off your old self, which is being
> corrupted by its deceitful desires; to be made new
> in the attitude of your minds; and to put on the
> new self, created to be like God in true righteous-
> ness and holiness. (Eph. 4:22–24 NIV)

After Katrina ravaged New Orleans, I went home to New Orleans with some guys from my church to gut some houses. We brought the oldest clothes we owned to work in the mold-infested houses each day. We brought old clothes because we knew we would throw them away at the end of each day.

After taking a shower each evening at the FEMA camp, I tossed the old clothes into trash bins throughout the camp. I loved the feel of putting on the new clothes my wife packed specifically for enjoying restaurants each night in the city.

After the shower I stayed away from the old clothes. I was now clean. I was refreshed, and I only wanted to wear the new clothes.

God has given you a new nature, a new set of clothes. He has given you His righteousness. Put that on. Leave the old clothes in the trash.

2. VIEW SIN AS SPIRITUAL ADULTERY

Sin is cheating on God.

As a pastor, I have counseled several couples struggling with the pain of infidelity. I have seen the hurt and despair in husbands and wives who are crushed because their spouses pursued excitement or intimacy with another. I have also seen the pain and regret in those who wandered, in those who strayed from the marriage relationship.

All would passionately say that adultery is never worth it.

And cheating on God is never worth it. Not only do we hurt God and harm our relationship with Him, but we also find ourselves empty. When God's people pursued other lovers, God said,

> For My people have committed a double evil:
> They have abandoned Me, the fountain of living
> water, and dug cisterns for themselves, cracked
> cisterns that cannot hold water. (Jer. 2:13)

When we choose to seek satisfaction and pleasure in things or people other than God, we commit spiritual adultery by chasing other lovers. And these other lovers cannot satisfy us because they are cracked cisterns. They are incapable of curing our thirst.

Seeking satisfaction anywhere other than in our relationship with Christ is essentially Chinese water torture. Chinese water torture was a cruel torture used on prisoners to drive them insane.

The prisoner is taken from his cell, thirsty and longing for water. His mouth is dry, and he craves water for his parched tongue. He is placed under a slow drip of water. The drop hits his forehead and the prisoner anxiously hopes the drop will run down the side of his face and into his dry mouth. But the drop slides off the side of his face. Of all the drops that hit the prisoner's forehead, few make it to his mouth. And the ones that make it to his mouth are insufficient to satisfy him. After hours of the slow dripping water, the drip no longer feels like a drip. Instead, the monotonous and consistent drip feels like a hammer hitting the prisoner's forehead.

The prisoner approaches the drip excited for the water but walks away still thirsty and in great pain. In the same way our pursuit of other lovers/gods brings pain and emptiness. Sin destroys, damages, and never quenches.

Only God can satisfy.

While we will not eliminate sin in this lifetime, we should develop an intense hatred for it because of the harm it does to our relationship with God. We should view sin as adultery that must be removed from our lives.

3. CONFESS

While we should seek to remove sin from our lives, we will still sin. While Christ has declared us perfect, practically we still live in our old and fallen bodies. While God's righteousness has been credited to us, we will not be without sin until heaven.

But what we do when we blow it is essential. How we respond to God as we sin is vital in our relationship with Him.

> If we say, "We have no sin," we are deceiving ourselves, and the truth is not in us. If we confess our sins, He is faithful and righteous to forgive us our sins and to cleanse us from all unrighteousness. If we say, "We have not sinned," we make Him a liar, and His word is not in us. My little children, I am writing you these things so that you may not sin. But if anyone does sin, we have an advocate with the Father—Jesus Christ the righteous One. (1 John 1:8–2:1)

This verse is very practical. Hate sin. But when you do sin, make things right with God. And you are able to make things right with God because Christ is your advocate. His death defends you. Constantly.

So why do I need to confess if God has already forgiven me?

Kaye and I have a great marriage, but it is not perfect. And sometimes we argue, discuss, debate. OK, we fight.

And we say things that are hurtful. We react in ways we should not. We offend each other.

Kaye has already forgiven me. I have already forgiven her. We are secure in our marriage. The relationship is not in jeopardy each time we argue. But the intimacy is harmed. So we always apologize.

When I blow it (and it's usually my fault even if it's not), I confess my failure to her and ask for her forgiveness. And our intimacy is restored.

While God has already forgiven you completely, confession restores your deep connection with Him. Confessing sin to God is not informing God you blew it as if He missed it, as if He does not already know. Confessing sin to God repairs the connection and allows Him to remove your guilt.

David's Example

David was passionate for God, yet he struggled with sin. His most famous sin was scandalous and involved adultery and murder. His fall began with being in the wrong place at the wrong time. As king, David should have been with his men in battle (2 Sam. 11:1). Instead, he was home alone and separated from the community of men who encouraged him.

One night he was bored and looking from his rooftop. He noticed a beautiful woman bathing. He sent some men to find out about her. When he learned she was Bathsheba, the wife of Uriah, he sent for her.

David committed adultery with her, getting her pregnant. The pattern of sin and deception continued as he attempted an elaborate cover-up. David called for Uriah to come home from the battle. When Uriah came to see David, David told him to go home, hoping he would sleep with his wife. Uriah was such a man of character that he did not go home; he slept outside the palace because his fellow soldiers were in battle.

David tried a second time; he got Uriah drunk. But on this night, Uriah slept outside his own house. Finally David asked his military leader to place Uriah on the front lines of battle where Uriah was killed.

God sent Nathan, the prophet, to confront David (2 Sam. 12). Nathan told David a story about a rich man who owned tons of sheep and a poor man who owned only one lamb. The rich man had a guest one night, and instead of killing one of his many sheep, he stole the one lamb from the poor man.

David burned with anger. Nathan said, "David, you are that man!" Nathan told David how disgusted God was and that the earthly consequences of the sin would be death for the child and calamity on the house of David.

But Nathan also told David, "The LORD has taken away your sin" (2 Sam. 12:13). David was already eternally forgiven because of his relationship with God, because David knew God and loved God.

But the physical and spiritual adultery harmed the deep connection and intimacy between David and God. David's guilt was eating away at his soul. He even hurt physically because of the distance in his relationship with God (Ps. 32:3–4).

So David approached God to restore the relationship. And when David confessed his sin and begged God for forgiveness, God removed the guilt (Ps. 32:5). The joy of David's relationship with God was restored to him (Ps. 51:12).

As His bride, continually seek His forgiveness so that you may enjoy the fullness of your relationship with God. Confess so that your connection and intimacy with God will be restored. And the sense of guilt taken away.

Consistent Confession

Don't be misled into thinking that the more you confess the further away from God you must be. The opposite is true. As your relationship with God becomes more intimate, confession is more prevalent. When Jesus gave us an example of prayer, He encouraged us to seek forgiveness:

> Therefore, you should pray like this: Our
> Father in heaven, Your name be honored as holy.
> Your kingdom come. Your will be done on earth as
> it is in heaven. Give us today our daily bread. *And*
> *forgive us our debts*, as we also have forgiven our
> debtors. And do not bring us into temptation,
> but deliver us from the evil one. (Matt. 6:9–13,
> emphasis added)

Notice the progression in the prayer. As you get closer to God (*Your name be honored as holy*), the more you confess because you increasingly realize His holiness. And the more you see Him for who He is, the more you realize how spiritually inadequate you are.

An inaccurate view of God leads to little or no confession. A reverent and accurate view of God leads to consistent confession. Consistent confession reveals a heart that is sensitive to God.

The person who consistently confesses sin is not the person who is far from God. The person who never confesses sin is the person who is far from God. His lack of pleas for forgiveness reveals he has a small view of God and a hardened heart toward sin.

There is a scene in *Talladega Nights* where Ricky Bobby (Will Ferrell's character) leads his family in prayer at the dinner table. In the scene Bobby prays to "baby Jesus." His wife interrupts his prayer to remind him that Jesus grew up, that He is not a baby any longer. Bobby insists on praying to 8-pound 6-ounce Baby Jesus. He says he likes that version of Jesus the best.

Many people like the image of Baby Jesus the best.

From that perspective Jesus in a manger is safe. Jesus as a baby is harmless. He is simply a cuddly infant to gawk over. He will not arise from the manger and ask for our devotion or life. He is simply a cute baby.

But this is not the image of Jesus presented in the Gospels. Even when Jesus was a baby, the magi (wise men) did not come to play. They came to worship (Matt. 2:11). They did not come to gawk. They came to fall facedown before God.

Jesus grew up. He is no longer in a manger. And He will not return to a manger. He is God. He is not merely a cute baby we pick up and play with. He is to be worshipped and feared. As C. S. Lewis pointed out in the Chronicles of Narnia, He is not safe. He is a lion, and our legs should tremble as we approach Him.

Because of his inaccurate view of Christ, Ricky Bobby never asked for forgiveness in his prayer.

David begged for forgiveness in his prayers because David viewed God as holy. David's longing to enjoy a close and intimate relationship with God drove him to confession. And God restored the intimacy between David and Himself.

David learned from his nighttime mistake on the rooftop. He later wrote to God, "On my bed I remember you; I think of you through the watches of the night" (Ps. 63:6 NIV). Instead of pursuing other lovers, David pursued God in the shadows of the night. He remembered God.

And he remembered that he was God's bride.

The reality: You are the bride of Christ.

The response: Remember you are His bride. View sin as adultery. And consistently confess.

Group Discussion Questions

Psalm 51 is a prayer of restoration and forgiveness. David prayed this beautiful prayer to God after being confronted by the prophet Nathan about his sin with Bathsheba. When we read Psalm 51, we are peering into David's personal prayer journal. As a group, read this prayer together and interact with the questions.

1. (Verses 1–2) What level of mercy does David long for? *Abundant*

2. (Verses 3–5) Is recognizing your sin essential for mercy? What does David say about his sin? *Yes, sinned against God.*

3. (Verses 6–9) What language does David use to express his desperation for forgiveness? *purge me with hyssop, renew, clean heart*

4. (Verses 10–12) Who creates a clean heart? From whom does salvation come?

    HS, God,

5. (Verses 13–15) After David has been shown mercy, what does he commit to do? *Declare praise,*

6. (Verses 16–17) What is God looking for in our hearts? What should our hearts be broken for?

    A broken and contrite heart,

    Our sin.

CHAPTER 5

||||||||||||||||||||||||

You Are His Servant

(belonging to God)

You are . . . a people belonging to God.

—1 PETER 2:9 NIV

P eople love job titles.

One corporate executive revealed to me that to keep employees happy, her company is overly generous with titles. The title "vice president" is attached to many positions. The corporate brass knows that titles motivate people. And it is easy to give a title to someone who is willing to work longer and harder for a new business card.

You have attended dinner parties where the first question after you introduce yourself is, "So what do you do?" Perhaps you struck up a conversation with a stranger on an airplane or at a restaurant. If you are really proud of your title, you could not wait to be asked, "What do you do?" If you want to end the conversation, just tell the person you are a pastor. Works for me every time.

Many people love titles because they find their identity in their title. Their title is more than a description of what they do. In their minds their title is a description of who they are.

My introduction to our obsession with job titles came during my first official job. Besides cutting lawns, my first job was at Bayou Animal Clinic, where I worked for a veterinarian. I took the job when I was fourteen to work a few days after school for $3.15 an hour, the going minimum wage at the time. I worked alongside a guy in his twenties who was really proud of the speakers in his old beat-up truck with tinted windows and his name sprayed on the back window. I think he worked just so he could continue dumping money into his truck. The rims and speakers were worth more than the truck itself.

When we first met, he introduced himself to me as the Kennel Assistant. Wow. Kennel Assistant sounded important, and since I was even younger, I would be the Associate Kennel Assistant.

As a fourteen-year-old, I was excited to know I had a cool title like Associate Kennel Assistant. After working a few days, I realized that a Kennel Assistant was a fancy title to describe someone who cleaned birdcages, fed cats, issued enemas to dogs, and picked up dog mess. The dirtiest tasks were delegated to the Associate, me.

Since we find much of our identity in our title, we tend to drift toward titles that make us sound important. Fancy titles give us a greater sense of identity. They contribute to our sense of self-worth.

What title should we be most proud to claim?

What title did the early Christians claim as their own?

Hi, I Am a Doulos

In the introduction in their letter to the Philippians, Paul and Timothy introduce themselves by their self-appointed title. Their title is not one the world would expect them to proudly proclaim. Paul and Timothy, two of Christianity's earliest and greatest leaders, introduce themselves with a lowly title. They begin their letter with a statement of their identity.

My Title

"Paul and Timothy, bondservants of Jesus Christ" (Phil. 1:1 NKJV). The word for bondservant in the original language is *doulos*, which literally means slave. A *doulos* is a slave who is willingly bound to another.

Hi, my name is Paul, and I am a slave of Christ Jesus. Good to meet you.

Hello, I am Timothy, a bondservant of Christ Jesus. What about you?

Paul and Timothy could have chosen other titles to describe their identity. Paul could have identified himself as the coauthor of half of the New Testament, the most popular book ever written. Or one of the greatest church leaders of all time. Timothy could have identified himself as one of Christianity's most influential young leaders.

But they chose the title *doulos*.

In the Jewish culture, someone who fell on hard times could choose to sell himself as a slave to someone. If a person was deep in debt, he could sell himself to the person whom he owed money. It was often a wise and logical choice because your master was required to take care of your needs and treat you well.

This was not slavery as we have imagined slavery; masters treated their servants as family. Many viewed selling themselves as servants as a viable option to provide for their family and survive.

God instituted a law among His people that the seventh year all debts would be completely forgiven. People who sold themselves to wealthy businessmen would be freed after six years of service. God gave instructions to His people detailing how to free servants who sold themselves into service.

> If a fellow Hebrew, a man or a woman, sells
> himself to you and serves you six years, in the
> seventh year you must let him go free. But if your
> servant says to you, "I do not want to leave you,"
> because he loves you and your family and is well
> off with you, then take an awl and push it through
> his ear lobe into the door, and he will become your
> servant for life. (Deut. 15:12, 16–17 NIV)

Servants were given the option to stay with their master, to continue in the service of the person who bought them. Many chose to stay because life with their master was so much better than life elsewhere. They loved the master and his family. They could not imagine living elsewhere. They could not imagine working for anyone else. So the servant could say, "I don't want to leave you. I want to stay."

At that point a special ceremony took place. The servant would place his ear against a door, and the master would take an awl, which is a small piercing device, and pierce the earlobe of the servant. Through this special ceremony the master and the servant entered into a special relationship, a bond that lasted their entire life. The servant was marked for life as the willing and grateful servant of his master.

The marking was important so that everyone who saw the servant and the master together would know that the servant chose to stay and serve. The servant was with his master out of love and gratitude, not obligation.

Like Paul and Timothy, you are a bondservant of Christ.

Before Christ you were ruined, bankrupt, and without hope. Yet Christ in His mercy purchased you and made you His own. He bought you not with silver or gold but with His own blood (1 Pet. 1:18–19). He gave you a new life, a home with Him, and a reason to live. He marked you as His own through the deposit of His Spirit into your life (Eph. 1:13).

And you stay with your Master because you love Him. While you serve because you love, you also know that true greatness is found in serving your Master.

Serving Is Greatness

One of the reasons bondservants chose to stay with their master was because life was so much better in the master's care. Perhaps sometimes bondservants would reflect on how life was before. . . .

They could remember how miserable the nights were hoping someone would let them stay in their home. They could recall how painful it was watching their children miss another meal. They could still feel the hopelessness and the emptiness. They remembered the embarrassment of wandering the streets at night with no place to go.

And life with their master, while not perfect, was so much better, so much more meaningful. Do you remember how empty life was away from your Master, apart from a relationship with God? Is not greatness found with your Master?

David cried to God, "Better is one day in your courts than a thousand elsewhere; I would rather be a doorkeeper in the house of my God than dwell in the tents of the wicked" (Ps. 84:10 NIV). David is saying, I would rather be a doorkeeper, a bouncer in God's house, than live large in the tents of the wicked because true greatness comes from serving God.

Unfortunately we sometimes forget that true greatness is serving our Master. We often suffer from memory loss as Christians, forgetting where greatness is found and living confused and misdirected lives.

In the movie *Memento*, the main character has an odd medical condition where he has no short-term memory. His wife was murdered, and he was injured during the attack. He can remember everything before the tragedy, but since the tragedy he has no short-term memory. His world is extremely confusing because in the middle of a conversation he forgets whom he is talking to, where he is, or why he is there.

Every few minutes he completely blanks out and starts over. To cope, he carries a Polaroid camera around with him and takes pictures of people he meets. He writes notes on the back of the photographs, telling himself whom he can and cannot trust. He tattoos important notes on his body, and he references the photographs and the markings on his body to navigate his every day life.

Tragically he trusts the wrong people and records incorrect markings on his body and on the Polaroid pictures. Because he relies so heavily on the notes he leaves for himself, he makes horrific decisions because he trusted the wrong people. He was marked by the wrong influences.

Do you ever live with memory loss, forgetting who you are?

Like the character in *Memento*, we often listen to the wrong voices and are marked by the wrong influences. When we are marked by the wrong influences, our daily lives are tragic attempts to please ourselves. The bombardment of messages telling us that we exist for ourselves contributes to our spiritual amnesia. And the messages detailing narcissistic methods to enjoy life are plentiful.

In recent years one of the most popular books in our culture is *The Secret*. The premise of the book is that you are the center of the universe, and you can attract all good things to yourself through your thoughts. The universe exists to serve you, and the secret is that you can attract greatness to yourself. In essence, you are your own god. So serve yourself. Jesus says the opposite. . . .

If anyone wants to be first, he must be last of all, and servant of all. (Mark 9:35)

Whoever wants to become great among you must be your servant, and whoever wants to be first among you must be a slave to all. For even the Son of Man did not come to be served, but to serve, and to give His life—a ransom for many. (Mark 10:43–45)

God's kingdom is an upside-down kingdom. In God's economy, true greatness comes from serving. For Jesus, *last is the new first*. If you choose to be a servant now, you will be first for all of eternity. If you choose to serve in this brief life, you will be rewarded for all of eternity.

Jesus did more than speak about serving; He lived the reality of His upside-down kingdom. He set the example for us.

The Example of Jesus

The biblical writers Peter and James joined Paul and Timothy in identifying themselves as servants. They opened their letters proudly bearing the title *doulos*, a bond servant of Christ.

Peter was one of Jesus' twelve disciples, so he saw firsthand the example of Jesus. He heard Jesus speak passionately about serving others. And he watched as Jesus lived His sermon. Peter learned from Jesus that serving is fundamentally Christian.

It was just before the Passover Feast. Jesus knew that the time had come for him to leave this world and go to the Father. Having loved his own who were in the world, he now showed them the full extent of his love. The evening meal was being served, and the devil had already prompted Judas Iscariot, son of Simon, to betray Jesus. Jesus knew

that the Father had put all things under his power,
and that he had come from God and was returning to God; so he got up from the meal, took off
his outer clothing, and wrapped a towel around his
waist. After that, he poured water into a basin and
began to wash his disciples' feet, drying them with
the towel that was wrapped around him.
(John 13:1–5 NIV)

The context of the story is the Passover so Jerusalem is
filled with Jewish people who have come to offer sacrifices
and to celebrate. Jesus decides to have a last supper with His
disciples. They observe the Passover meal and Jesus intro-
duces a new symbolism to the meal with the cup representing His blood and the bread representing His body.

According to the other Gospel accounts, Jesus is
having the meal in a borrowed upper room. All twelve of
the disciples are present, including Judas, who has already
agreed to betray Jesus. If the room were not borrowed,
hosts would have been present, and a servant would have
been provided. The servant would have been responsible
to wash the feet of the guests. Washing feet was reserved
for the lowest slave on the organizational chart, the newbie
or the youngest.

Because of the Passover, there were tons of Jewish people in Jerusalem for the celebration. There were no paved
roads. With so many people walking through the streets, the
roads were filthy. Nike cofounder Phil Knight would not be
born for another two thousand years so the disciples did not
sport shoes with a swoosh. Or any other shoes. They wore
sandals. Thus the feet of the disciples were disgusting. Since
they reclined to eat around a low table, the odor must have
been rank.

During the meal the disciples argue about who is the greatest (Luke 22:24).

He was teaching them With the argument as background music, Jesus gets up from the meal. He must have been disappointed because He constantly taught the disciples that true greatness comes from serving. Yet none of them stood up to do what needed to be done.

Jesus takes off His outer robe and wraps the servant's towel around His waist. He kneels before His disciples and washes their feet. The hands that created the world washes feet. The hands that fashioned humanity rubs dirt off grungy and nasty feet. God is on His knees cleaning the feet of His twelve disciples.

Including Judas.

Jesus washes the feet of the person who would betray Him in a few hours. And Jesus knew it. Yet Jesus kneels before Judas and rubs the dirt off his toes.

When He finishes washing their feet, He puts on His clothes and returns to His place and says:

> Do you understand what I have done for you? You call me "Teacher" and "Lord," and rightly so, for that is what I am. Now that I, your Lord and Teacher, have washed your feet, you also should wash one another's feet. I have set you an example that you should do as I have done for you. I tell you the truth, no servant is greater than his master, nor is a messenger greater than the one who sent him. *Now that you know these things, you will be blessed if you do them.* (John 13:12–17 NIV, emphasis added)

The apostle John recorded the account of Jesus' washing the disciples' feet. John's Gospel is the only Gospel that *Hu!* does not record any of Jesus' parables. To John, all of Jesus' life was a parable, a teachable moment. And God washing feet was the ultimate parable on serving.

As a follower of Christ, you are challenged to wash feet. Not literally, but figuratively. Christ asks you to serve others, to embrace your identity as a servant. He has handed you a towel and has given you a basin.

Servants serve. A nonserving Christian is an oxymoron just like white chocolate, tall midget, fast turtle, and country music. You are a servant. So serve.

Now that you know these things, you will be blessed if you do them.

The Serving High

Jesus told His disciples that they would be blessed if they served. And you will be blessed if you serve, both eternally and presently. Eternally you will receive rewards because of your faithful service. Presently, a supernatural high comes with serving.

Experiencing God overflow out of your life to serve others trumps anything the world has to offer. There is a blessing in serving that cannot be experienced any other way.

For my birthday one year, my staff gave me tickets to opening night of the Miami Heat season. Kaye and I went to the game together. It was an electric atmosphere. The arena was jumping.

The scene was in stark contrast to the Midnight all-stars city league I play in. We are not all-stars, nor do we play at midnight, but we do love to play. Only a few people are in the stands to watch our games, mainly wives graciously watching our attempts to relive our high school glory days. Sometimes players help prepare the gym by moving equipment off the floor. The refs show up five minutes before game time.

Yet playing is much better than watching, even on opening night.

Before each game, my adrenaline is pumping. I stretch at home, choose my lucky socks, and mentally prepare for the game. While many would say the games were meaningless, they were not to my teammates or me. We were thrilled to be in the game.

Playing brings a greater high than watching. In the same way, serving always provides a greater blessing than sitting. Unfortunately many Christians forsake the serving high to sit and observe. Statistics tell us that the majority of "Christians" never get in the game. Instead they choose to be spectators to the work of God.

People who opt out of serving remind me of Michal.

MICHAL'S STORY

Michal is married to David, the king of Israel. Together they live in Jerusalem, and their city is about to change. The ark of the covenant is returning to their city. The ark was a big deal to the Jewish people. It was a big deal period. It was where God and man met (remember the chapter on being a priest). The return of the ark was a significant occasion for the people, both spiritually and nationally.

When those who were carrying the ark of the
LORD had taken six steps, he sacrificed a bull and a
fattened calf. David, wearing a linen ephod, danced
before the LORD with all his might, while he and
the entire house of Israel brought up the ark of
the LORD with shouts and the sound of trumpets.
(2 Sam. 6:13–15 NIV)

This was a huge day. Adrenaline was pumping. People
were shouting. Music was bumping. The king was dancing.
The atmosphere was electric because the glory of God was
coming into their city!

So the *entire* house of Israel was involved.

Everyone was thrilled to participate with what God
was doing. Everyone wanted to contribute. Because David
was fanatical about music, tons of people played instru-
ments and sang. The Jewish historian, Josephus, wrote
that there were seven choirs assembled before David in the
procession. Some carried the ark. Others helped with food
preparation and distribution. There were numerous opportunities to serve. And the *entire house* of Israel was tapped
into the joyful celebration.

Everyone except Michal.

As the ark of the LORD was entering the City
of David, Michal daughter of Saul watched from
a window. And when she saw King David leaping
and dancing before the LORD, she despised him in
her heart. (2 Sam. 6:16 NIV)

Michal watched. She observed from a window while
others served. She watched, abandoning the opportunity
to be a part of something great. Michal was a spiritual

moocher. She was going to reap the benefits from God's presence in her city without contributing.

Michal watched the day happen in the comfort of her home. And her day ended in misery. Bitterness fumed in her heart. Is there not a relationship between bitterness and self-consumption?

Bleacher Christians are miserable people. Because Jesus knows this, He says with confidence, *Now that you know these things, you will be blessed if you do them.*

If you do them . . .

How does someone live the reality of a servant? What does it look like to get out of the bleachers and into the game?

1. SERVE THE MASTER'S FAMILY

The bond servant chose to stay with his master because he loved him. He wanted to express his love continually through his service because service is the full extent of love. When Jesus washed His disciples' feet, He was "show[ing] them the full extent of his love" (John 13:1 NIV).

The servant's service to the master was often manifested in service to the master's family. Bond servants only stayed if they loved not only the master but his family as well (Deut. 15:16).

Servants would provide care for the master's children and protect the family. Perhaps they would help the kids get ready for school in the morning, assist them with their homework, and check the security of the home each night. Perhaps the bond servant would play games with the family each evening, pray with the family, and celebrate holidays with the family.

While God desires for you to serve the world around you, the Master also asks you to serve His family. And the church is God's family. By "church," I mean God's people, not a building, denomination, creed, confession, or organization. The church is the gathering of the Master's family in specific locations all around the world.

Wait a second! What just happened?

Am I actually suggesting that we invest our time serving the church? Do I have the audacity to equate serving the church with serving Christ?

You may be saying, "I want to serve Christ but not the church. I love Jesus but not the church." If so, I understand. I once felt the same way.

Early in my faith, and even early in ministry, I was cynical and frustrated with the church. I remember visiting a church with some friends just to bash their newly renovated church sanctuary. When we saw the expensive chandeliers and opulent decorations, we talked negatively about the church over lunch. *They could build a church in the Yucatan for every one of those chandeliers.*

I remember being scolded by a gaudily dressed woman with bad breath at a church because I painted the youth room for the teenagers. She informed me that the building and grounds committee was upset because I corrupted their beautiful white walls. I complained that if church people's greatest mission was to keep their walls clean, then they missed the entire point of the gospel.

When I started preaching, I viewed every sermon as an opportunity to unload on church people for being unloving to the lost world around them. I was convinced that I could be deeply committed to Christ but adamantly frustrated and opposed to church.

Then I got married.

God used my marriage to change my heart. Not only because Kaye seasoned me with some mercy and compassion but also because I began to understand the relationship between a husband and a wife.

God calls the church His bride.

God chooses the image of marriage to describe His love for the church. I realized that loving Jesus but not His church would be like someone coming to me and saying, "I like you, but I cannot stand your wife." Insisting the church was ridiculous and not worthy of my service would be like someone ridiculing my wife and expecting me to be OK with it.

I am not saying the church is perfect. I know my church is not perfect because I am a part of it. However, I am saying that the church is the bride of Christ, that the church is the family of the Master. And the Master asks us to serve His family.

God has given you a spiritual gift, and one of the reasons for your gifting is so that God's family will benefit from your contribution. The family suffers if you choose not to serve. The family suffers if you forget you are a marked servant.

2. MANAGE GOD'S GRACE

In the Jewish culture, the master would entrust specific responsibilities to his servant. The servant may be responsible for managing some aspect of the master's business or administering a portion of the family land. The servant would be honored to manage the resources or possessions of the master.

Serving is management of God's grace. The Scripture reads, "Each one should use whatever gift he has received to serve others, *faithfully administering* God's grace in its various forms" (1 Pet. 4:10 NIV, emphasis added).

Administering God's grace?

Since we are God's servants, He has entrusted us with His resources. We are His stewards, His managers, His administrators. Not only do we manage God's finances, creation, and time; but we also manage His grace.

God has entrusted His grace to you for you to manage. When you serve, you administer God's grace to other people. As you serve others, you dispense God's love and compassion. You are the manager of God's greatest resource—His grace. And you are responsible to administer it through serving.

So do not take serving God lightly. Faithfulness is essential.

3. ENJOY YOUR UNIQUE CONTRIBUTION

As God's bond servant, your service is unique. Your contribution to the Master's kingdom and family is uniquely customized to your calling, personality, gifting, and stage of life. In other words, you administer God's grace through your unique gifting.

> Each one should use *whatever gift* he has
> received to serve others, faithfully administering
> God's grace in its *various forms*. If anyone speaks,
> he should do it as one speaking the very words of
> God. If anyone serves, he should do it with the
> strength God provides, so that in all things God

may be praised through Jesus Christ. To him be
the glory and the power for ever and ever. Amen.
(1 Pet. 4:10–11 NIV, emphasis added).

While God's grace is administered through His servants, His grace is administered in various forms. Because
we are different, with unique spiritual gifts, God's mercy is
expressed in a variety of ways.

One weekend I taught this principle to the people in
our church. I emphasized that God's grace is like water:
purifying and refreshing. And we are honored to administer
His grace. To illustrate, a myriad of water dispensers were
placed on the platform.

Perhaps God has gifted you to be a sprinkler. You
spread God's grace to a lot of people in small ways. Perhaps
God has gifted you to be a watering pot. You nurture a
group of people over time. Or maybe God has gifted you
to be a pitcher. You refresh people with hospitality and
tangible acts of service. Perhaps God has gifted you to be a
pressure cleaner. You bring change and leadership into situations that need a fresh touch of God's grace. Maybe God
has gifted you to be a dropper. You think your contribution
is small, but your contribution is essential.

There is a unique contribution that only you can
make. There is a specific way that God's grace is going
to be distributed through you. Each of us plays a critical
role in God's desire to reveal His glory through the church
(Eph. 3:10), and your Master desires your unique and specific contribution.

Check Your Mark

After six years the master knocks on the room of the servant one evening. The master has put off the conversation for weeks but knows he must free his servant. He sits down, and the conversation begins with an awkward pause.

I appreciate what you have done for me, but you have served me for six years. You are now free to go.

The servant has anticipated the conversation because he knows the law as well. He already has the response formulated in his mind. . . .

Master, I do not want to leave you. Where else would I go? I love you and your family. I want to stay with you for the rest of my life. I want everyone to know that I am your servant and I am bound to you for the rest of my life. I am going to serve your family faithfully.

Together the master and servant walk to the tool room. The master takes the awl and pierces the servant's ear, marking him. The two embrace, and their relationship is now deeper than ever before. The marking proves that the servant is with the master willingly, serving out of love and not mere obligation.

The master served the servant by adopting him as a family member. The expression of love forever marked the servant. The servant agreed to be marked externally because he was already marked internally through the relationship to his master.

In the same way the foundation of Christ's command for us to serve others is that He has served us. He told His disciples, "Now that I, your Lord and Teacher, have washed your feet, you also should wash one another's feet" (John 13:14 NIV).

What Christ did for His disciples in the upper room is a snapshot of what He has done for us. He took off His royal robes, humbled Himself, stooped down to our level, placed Himself in a human body, and served us by dying for us (Phil. 2:5–8). Just as the master rescued the servant from a hopeless existence, our Master has rescued us.

He asks us to serve others in response to His service to us.

The early Christians kept calling themselves a *doulos* in their letters to churches. They proudly bore the title of bond servant. They embraced the identity of a servant, and their identity impacted how they lived.

Are you proud to be a bond servant of Christ? Or do you prefer another title?

The reality: You are a servant.

The response: Serve the Master.

Group Discussion Questions

1. What would make a servant desire to stay with a master in the Jewish culture? How does this compare to our relationship with God?

   He becomes like family. We don't just go to work and come home, we always are with God, he is home is here every day.

2. What types of messages cause us to forget that true greatness comes from being a servant?

   How can we get more people without going away?

3. Read the story of David and Michal in 2 Samuel 6:13–21. What characteristics of a servant do you find in David?

   Worshipful, sacrificial.

4. How has Christ served you (washed your feet)?

   Died on Cross, Given me a blessed life, I DIE

5. As a group, define "the church." Do you agree that Christ desires us to serve the church?

   The people of God. Yes.

6. What excuses do people give for not serving? Are any of these valid?

   No. *"I'm tired spiritually." "I don't know what God needs"*

7. Give some personal examples of the tangible blessings that come from serving.

   - Experience.
   - Spiritual Highs
   - Leadership

   -

CHAPTER 6

You Are God's Friend
(people of God)

Best of all God is with us.

—JOHN WESLEY

M iami has the highest percentage of weird people per capita in the entire world. While I do not have the empirical data to back such a statement, casual observation and many personal case studies give me confidence to make the bold claim.

One night after our Saturday night church service, a guy approached me wanting to talk. We sat down at one of our café tables, and he told me about the night he saw Jesus in a spaceship.

Yes. Jesus in a spaceship.

I asked him what he was shooting, dropping, smoking, or snorting the night he thinks he saw Jesus in a spaceship. He assured me he was completely clean when a spaceship hovered over his house. According to him, the door opened, and Jesus was staring at him from the spaceship.

What does Jesus look like?

He insisted that Jesus is a white guy with palm trees protruding from his scalp. I told him that Jesus is Jewish and that there was no biblical evidence to suggest Jesus would sport palm tree dreadlocks. Or need a spaceship.

Noticeably frustrated with my disbelief, the story immediately escalated. He told me that every single night Jesus pulls into his celestial driveway in his decked out spaceship. And every night Jesus opens the spaceship doors and strikes up a conversation.

Our conversation ended when I asked him if I could come to his house and observe the phenomenon. He simply walked away.

While Jesus does not cruise around in spaceships, He does want a deep friendship with His followers. While Jesus will not physically hover above your house, He does desire to enjoy a close relationship with you. While Jesus will not stare at you with palm trees flowing from His scalp, He does desire to speak to your life.

He views you as His friend.

The famous minister John Wesley was surrounded with his closest friends when he was on his deathbed. He called his friends close to him as he breathed his last words. His final words were. "Best of all, God is with us."

Best of all, God is with us.

Years before Jesus was born, Isaiah prophesied that the Messiah would be born of a virgin, and that He would be called Immanuel (Isa. 7:14). Jesus is Immanuel, which means "God with us" (Matt. 1:23). Jesus was His common name, but Immanuel is the reality of who He is. He is with us.

We often view the Christian life as being *about God*. Or we do things *for God*. Or we approach life as a way to get *to God*. Yet God desires us to be *with God*.

With us is God's heart.

Dinner with God

While on this earth, Jesus spent a lot of time at a house in Bethany where two sisters, Mary and Martha lived. One day Jesus visited for dinner.

for not with

> As Jesus and his disciples were on their way, he came to a village where a woman named Martha opened her home to him. She had a sister called Mary, who sat at the Lord's feet listening to what he said. But Martha was distracted by all the preparations that had to be made. She came to him and asked, "Lord, don't you care that my sister has left me to do the work by myself? Tell her to help me!"
> "Martha, Martha," the Lord answered, "you are worried and upset about many things, but only one thing is needed. Mary has chosen what is better, and it will not be taken away from her." (Luke 10:38–42 NIV)

Jesus comes to the house to be with Mary and Martha. He plops down tired from walking, and Mary sits at His feet. Martha gets extremely frustrated. Martha is producing an elaborate meal and there are some unfinished tasks. She yelled at Jesus, *Tell her to help me!*

Awkward moment. Martha just yelled at God.

Jesus literally says to Martha, *Martha you are worried about all these dishes of food, all these preparations for the meal, but only one portion of the meal is necessary. The best part of the meal is not the turkey or the dressing. I am the best portion of the meal.*

Martha was too busy doing things *for* Jesus to be still and be *with* Him. She was more occupied with her cause than she was with Christ. Mary, however, savored the opportunity to be *with* God.

Martha viewed the evening as dinner *for* God.

Mary viewed the evening as dinner *with* God.

One of my favorite restaurants is Outback Steakhouse. When we lived in Ohio, Kaye and I enjoyed an Outback ritual on many Saturdays. We would skip lunch and go to Outback at 4:00 before the evening crowd arrived. By the time we sat down to eat, I was starving. I was dreaming of a filet mignon all day, but I could not wait to eat any longer. So we would order the Bloomin' Onion and insist the server bring us some more bread. I would literally devour the Bloomin' Onion and almost inhale the bread.

By the time the steak arrived, I was no longer hungry. I filled up on the cheap stuff. I was too full to enjoy the best part of the meal, the part of the meal that pulled me into the restaurant in the first place.

Jesus told Martha that He was the best part of the meal. Mary enjoyed the best part of the meal. Martha filled up on the cheap stuff.

If you are not hungry for a close friendship with God, you are probably filling up on the cheap stuff of life. If you are not hungry to sit at the feet of Jesus, as Mary did, perhaps you are devouring parts of life that will never truly satisfy.

The one thing that is needed is Christ. A close friendship *with* Him is all that is necessary.

More than Servants

In John 13, Jesus washes His disciples' feet, holding high the value of serving. He challenges them to embrace their identity as servants (the previous chapter). Moments later Jesus tells His disciples that they are more than servants. He calls them friends.

> Greater love has no one than this, that he lay down his life for his friends. You are my friends if you do what I command. I no longer call you servants because a servant does not know his master's business. Instead I have called you friends, for everything that I learned from my Father I have made known to you. (John 15:13–15 NIV)

When Jesus proclaims His eternal friendship to His disciples, Judas is noticeably missing. Before Jesus assured the disciples of their eternal friendship, Jesus asked His betrayer to leave. In other words, Jesus does not toss the friendship word around lightly.

Yet He calls you His friend.

What does it mean to be a friend of God?

He Shares His Thoughts

We share our thoughts with our friends.

When I asked Kaye to marry me, I pulled my friends into the conversation. I shared my plans with them because they were my friends. My roommate helped plan the night, even coming out from behind a tree with a guitar to sing as my singing would have ruined the night.

When Kaye and I were praying for a child, we shared our thoughts with our friends in our small group. We discussed our struggle, our hopes, and our frustrations. Because of friendship, we did not hide our thoughts from our friends.

In the Scripture, Abraham is called a friend of God several times (James 2:23; 2 Chron. 20:7). And as God's friend, God shared His thoughts with Abraham. This truth is evident in one of the most well-known stories in the Bible, the story of Sodom and Gomorrah (Gen. 18).

God sent some angels to tell Abraham that he and his wife are having a child, which was a huge miracle because of their age. And as the angels are leaving, God decides to disclose even more information to Abraham.

God is ready to wipe out Sodom and Gomorrah for all their wickedness. But before He does, God actually shares His thoughts with Abraham. The Lord said, "Shall I hide from Abraham what I am about to do?" (Gen. 18:17 NIV). God invites Abraham into a conversation about His plans.

Why does God share His plans with Abraham?

Does God need Abe's advice? Is God confused and looking for someone to bounce His ideas off of? Does God lie down on Abraham's couch looking for wise counsel?

Is God wanting to have His feelings validated? Is God uncertain about His decision?

Or does God share His thoughts with Abraham simply because they are friends?

Jesus says to you, "You are My friend. And because you are My friend, I share with you all My Father's business." As God's friend, you are in His inner circle. He shares His thoughts with you.

The depth of our friendship with God is difficult to grasp.

After all, I have never experienced God's voice like Abraham did. He has never sent angels to tell me I am going to be a daddy. He has never pulled me aside and told me He is planning to blow up a city. And I have not hung out with Jesus like the disciples. They were right there with Him when He called them friends. It's not the same for me.

According to Jesus, it's better. Jesus indicated we would enjoy a deeper friendship with God than Abraham or the disciples.

Moments after telling the disciples they were His friends, Jesus told them that it was best for them if He left the world because when He left, He would send the Holy Spirit to be their counselor and teacher. And the Holy Spirit would always be with them, always teaching them, always sharing with them everything from the Father.

I have much more to say to you, more than
you can now bear. But when he, the Spirit of truth,
comes, he will guide you into all truth. He will
not speak on his own; he will speak only what he
hears, and he will tell you what is yet to come. He

will bring glory to me by taking from what is mine
and making it known to you. (John 16:12–14 NIV)

As a Christian, you have the Holy Spirit of God living
inside of you. The Holy Spirit takes the thoughts of God
and makes them known to you. He speaks truth into your
life. He guides you. He never misleads you because He does
not speak on His own. He only speaks from the mind and
heart of God. You are God's friend, and the Holy Spirit
constantly shares God's thoughts with you because He never
leaves you.

You are not like Abraham who enjoys a conversation
with God only to leave the presence of God. You are not
like the disciples who enjoy the presence of God only when
standing close to Christ. Your friendship can be deeper. He
is always speaking, always guiding, always leading.

LISTENING 101

But how do you know you are hearing His voice? How
can you be sure you are hearing His thoughts?

The first test is: *Does what you think God is saying
to you line up with what He has already said in Scripture?*
God will never pull you in a direction that is contrary to
Scripture.

God gets blamed for a lot of things, such as spaceships and palm tree haircuts. Just because you ate too much
Mexican food and feel a little funny does not mean God is
speaking to you.

A guy recently told me that he thought God wanted
him to leave his wife for another woman. He just was not
happy and he reasoned that God wanted him to be happy.
God will never share thoughts with you that are contrary

to His Word. If you sense something that is contrary to Scripture, it is not God's voice you are hearing.

But what if Scripture does not speak directly to your decision? No verse in the Bible tells you whom to marry or where to live or what job to accept.

Jesus said the Holy Spirit *will* guide you in all truth. If you will listen to Him, He will share His thoughts with you. He does not hold His thoughts from you. You are His friend and through His Holy Spirit, who lives in you, He speaks to your spirit, to your heart.

We all have friends who don't listen very well, friends who talk too much. Friends who are story-toppers, who can always trump a story with a bigger and better story. Friends whose calls you screen unless you have an hour to spare. Friends who talk over you, who constantly interrupt even when you are simply answering a question they asked.

While we love these people because they are our friends, conversations with them are extremely frustrating.

I wonder if God ever feels the same about us.

Will we ever stop talking to listen? Instead of listening, our prayers are often long run-on sentences with no commas and no pauses. God speaks to us, wanting to share His thoughts, but we often talk over Him.

As His friend, listen.

He shares His thoughts with you. And He shows His greatness to you.

He Shows His Greatness

When something great happens in our lives, we call our friends. If we have great news to share, we tell our friends. Moses enjoyed a close friendship with God, and God showed Moses His greatness.

> The LORD would speak to Moses face to face, as a man speaks with his friend. . . . Then Moses said, "Now show me your glory." And the LORD said, "I will cause all my goodness to pass in front of you, and I will proclaim my name, the LORD, in your presence. I will have mercy on whom I will have mercy, and I will have compassion on whom I will have compassion. But," he said, "you cannot see my face, for no one may see me and live." (Exod. 33:11, 18–20 NIV)

Obviously the language about Moses speaking face-to-face with God is imagery because just a few verses later God tells Moses that no one can see His face. But the imagery is powerful and illustrates the close friendship Moses and God enjoyed. Moses would talk to God as a friend.

And because of their close friendship, Moses asked God to show him His glory, the greatness of all His attributes. Amazingly God agreed. God put Moses in the cleft of the rock and let Moses see the backside of His glory.

Jesus says you are His friend. He has great things to show you. He desires continually to reveal His greatness to you, just as He did with Moses.

I fear we often live bland and boring lives because we don't press in and enjoy a friendship with God that brings us to the point of asking God to show us His glory. I fear we miss out on the greatness of God because we pray small prayers and attempt small things for God.

I want to pray "God, show me Your glory" type of prayers and not mild and tame "help me have a good day" kind of prayers. I want to be such close friends with Christ that He is constantly showing me His greatness. I want to be a part of big things for God, things that can only be attributed to the greatness of God.

Elijah was a man who was deeply committed to God. He enjoyed a close friendship with God, one where he saw the greatness of God displayed. His story inspires me. . . .

ELIJAH'S STORY

Elijah is a prophet who speaks for God to God's people. Elijah is distressed and burdened because his country is littered with little "g" gods. The people have shifted their hearts away from God toward idols. Altars to Baal and Asherah poles had been set up. Baal was supposedly the god in charge of the weather. He was the most famous god. Astoreth was the female equivalent of Baal. So the people built these huge poles, known as Asherah poles to worship her.

All of this has happened under King Ahab's watch. Ahab is the king of Israel. The Bible says he did more to provoke the Lord than any of the other kings before him (1 Kings 16:33). Ahab was not a murderer, a thief, or an adulterer. He promoted the worship of other gods, and this infuriates God.

God's response is awesome and ironic. Because these little "g" gods were supposedly in charge of the weather, God causes there to be a drought for three years.

The country is in a drought. The farmers and the professional landscapers are upset because their business has tanked. Ahab has letters on his desk from every home owners association in the country. The water conservationists are livid. No one is happy. People are desperate for rain and are willing to worship any god who is able to send it.

To prove that God is God, Elijah calls for the ultimate showdown: God vs. gods. Elijah challenges Ahab to gather the 450 prophets of Baal and the 400 prophets of the Asherah. Instead of 3:00 in the school parking lot, Elijah names Mt. Carmel as the location for the battle. A huge crowd gathers to watch 850 prophets of lowercase "g" gods and one prophet of God.

Mt. Carmel was typically a place where plants, fruit, and vegetation grew in abundance. But not at this time. By choosing the showdown to take place on Mt. Carmel, Elijah was insisting that the people be confronted with the worst images of the drought.

Elijah gives the rules for the showdown. The prophets of Baal will put a sacrifice on an altar, and Elijah will put a sacrifice on the altar. Each group will set up their altar and then call on their god to light it on fire. The God who answers is God. Sounds fair to the prophets of Baal and Asherah because their gods are supposed to be in charge of the weather.

The prophets of Baal dance around the altar all day long. They cut themselves. They yell to their god. Nothing happens. No fire from heaven.

Elijah engages in some trash talking. *Cry louder. Maybe your god is sleeping. Maybe he is thinking.* "But there was no response, no one answered, no one paid attention" (1 Kings 18:29).

Then Elijah steps up. He calls the people to him so they can see what is about to happen. He repairs the altar of the Lord and places the sacrifice on the altar. And then he digs a trench around the altar.

Elijah asks people to pour water all over the altar. Again. And again. So much water is poured on the altar that the trench surrounding the altar is filled. Elijah steps forward and prays:

> "O LORD, God of Abraham, Isaac and Israel,
> let it be known today that you are God in Israel
> and that I am your servant and have done all these
> things at your command. Answer me, O LORD,
> answer me, so these people will know that you,
> O LORD, are God, and that you are turning their
> hearts back again." Then the fire of the LORD fell
> and burned up the sacrifice, the wood, the stones
> and the soil, and also licked up the water in the
> trench. When all the people saw this, they fell
> prostrate and cried, "The LORD—he is God! The
> LORD—he is God!" (1 Kings 18:36–39 NIV)

What a moment! The half-naked and bleeding prophets of Baal were probably speechless. Besides being hoarse from all their yelling, their impotent god gets spanked in front of all the people. The fire of God fell.

But why did Elijah pour water on the altar? In the middle of a drought?

Elijah poured water on the altar so it would be clear that it was God who lit everything on fire. So that no one could say, *I think because of the drought that perhaps some heat from one of the stones caused a piece of straw to catch on fire and then that just spread.* Elijah poured water all over the altar so the fire would have no explanation other than God.

God is attracted to situations where it will be clear that He is the one who intervened. God is attracted to situations

where His friends sincerely ask for His greatness and glory
to be displayed.

Perhaps you need to pour some water on a situation in
your life. Perhaps you need to give up, release control, and
allow your Friend to fight the battle. And when God's greatness is revealed, people will say, "The LORD—he is God!"

As your friend, God shares His thoughts with you,
shows His greatness to you, and He includes you in His
plans.

He Includes You

We include our friends in our plans, in our lives. When
someone gives you great seats to a game, you think of
friends you can invite. When Memorial Day or Labor Day
rolls around, you include your friends in the plans for the
cookout. You could go to the game alone. You could cookout alone. You don't need to include your friends. But you
do because you want to.

Jesus declares that as His friend, you know the Father's
business (John 15:15). You are included in God's plan. God
does not need us. He could go to the game alone. He is
completely sufficient in Himself, yet He chooses to include
us in His plans.

From the beginning of humanity, God has included His
friends in His plans. God has continually entrusted responsibility to people. Early in the story of humanity, we see God
including us. . . .

So the Lord God formed out of the ground
each wild animal and each bird of the sky, and

brought each to the man to see what he would call
it. And whatever the man called a living creature,
that was its name. (Gen. 2:19)

God has just created the earth and everything in it. He
now decides He is going to bring the animals to Adam, for
Adam to name. He gives the responsibility of naming the
animals to Adam.

Why did God do that? Was God tired and out of
energy? Had the entire creation process sapped God's
energy? Were His creative juices running low? Or did He
simply enjoy partnering with Adam on the significant and
enjoyable process of naming animals?

God and Adam shared an incredible day together.
God brought each animal to Adam, and Adam named the
animal. From the dawn of humanity, God has delighted in
including His friends in His work, in His life.

The only miracle recorded in all four Gospels is the
famous story of Jesus feeding five thousand people with two
fish and five loaves of bread. There is a huge crowd walking around with Jesus. Jesus teaches them along the way. It
gets late in the day, and the disciples suggest that Jesus send
the crowd away so they can go crash a local Bennigan's or
Applebee's.

Jesus asks Philip where the closest bread store is
located. Philip did the math in his head and pointed out that
it would take eight month's salary to feed everyone.

Jesus was asking Philip a rhetorical question. Jesus
knew what He was planning to do; He was simply testing
Philip (John 6:6). He did not need a brainstorming session
with the disciples.

His question was an invitation.

Jesus asks the disciples where they will get food because He wants to include them. He wants to partner with them to serve the people.

Andrew finds a boy who has two fish and five loaves of bread. Jesus transforms the kid's lunch into enough food to feed the entire crowd. And the disciples are included in the miracle. They pass out the food to the people.

After everyone eats, Jesus asks the disciples to gather all the leftovers. The disciples gather the leftovers into food baskets. There are precisely twelve baskets worth of leftovers, one for each disciple.

As your friend, Jesus seeks to include you in His plans. Even in small ways. For the disciples, passing out fish and chips increased their faith and allowed them to participate in God's miracle.

You are God's friend. He shares His thoughts with you. He shows His greatness to you. And He includes you in His plans. How should you respond to this reality?

Enjoy Being with God

Mary and Martha, the two sisters in Bethany, had a brother named Lazarus. Jesus and Lazarus were evidently very close (John 11:3). Jesus hears one day that Lazarus is sick. The sisters sent word to Jesus, hoping He would rush to Bethany to heal Lazarus.

Jesus waits until Lazarus has been dead four days before arriving in Bethany. Martha runs out to meet Jesus. *Jesus if you had been here, my brother would not have died.* Jesus tells her that Lazarus would rise again.

Jesus walks to the tomb and yells, "Lazarus, come out!" (John 11:43).

He calls Lazarus by name. And Lazarus walks out of the tomb. Alive. The crowd helps take off the grave clothes, and Lazarus has a new shot at life.

The next chapter in the Gospel of John tells the story of another meal at Mary and Martha's house. Lazarus was at the dinner party, reclining at the table *with* Jesus (John 12:2). I imagine the conversation around the dinner table was entertaining. *Hey Lazarus, tell it to us one more time. . . .*

Lazarus was reclining at the table *with* Jesus. Where else would he be? Jesus raised him from the dead! Of course he was going to be sitting close to Jesus.

Like Lazarus, you were spiritually dead in sin. But Christ has made you alive. He has given you a new life. Where else will you be other than *with* Jesus?

Because you are His friend, simply enjoy being *with* Him.

View your spiritual journey as a journey *with* God, not *toward* Him. View your daily life as an opportunity to live *with* God, not simply *for* God. Go to work *with* Him. Enjoy your leisure time *with* God.

Because Jesus is Immanuel, the message of the gospel is not about doing things *for* God or to get *to* God. Live life as dinner *with* Jesus instead of dinner *for* Him. The bottom line is an intimate relationship *with* God.

Best of all God is with us.

The reality: you are God's friend.

The response: live with Him.

Group Discussion Questions

1. What are some important qualities you look for in a friend? As a group, come up with a list of essential qualities in a good friend. *- Trustworthy - Reliable, - Deeper level*

2. How does Jesus exemplify the essential qualities of a friend? *Came to earth as a human + can't sin,*

3. How do you listen to God's voice? How have you learned to hear His voice? *- Prayer + Like ours! - Line up w/ Scripture*

4. What are some practical ways God includes us in His plans? *- Discipling - miracle - converting*

5. What is the difference between viewing the Christian life as "dinner for God" or "dinner with God"? Which view describes your approach? *② Probably DFG. ① Living for to Live with.*

6. How should being a friend of God impact your approach to spiritual growth? *Talk more openly, Listen more openly, pray boldly*

7. Spend several minutes as a small group being still, listening to God in personal prayer and reflection.

CHAPTER 7

You Are an Alien

(alien + stranger)

I urge you, as aliens and strangers.

—1 PETER 2:11 NIV

In the movie *Unknown*, five people wake up in a chemical warehouse with no recollection of who they are or how they got there. Weapons are lying on the ground. One of them is tied up. There is no escape from the warehouse.

Several of them search for clues in the warehouse, seeking to discover who they are and why they are there. They find a police officer dead in a closet. They also find a newspaper and realize that two of them are kidnapped police officers and three of them are kidnappers. But they don't know who is who.

They remember nothing from their past, nothing from their childhood. They cannot recall how they got to the warehouse. No one even knows his own name. After a phone call to the warehouse, they realize that the rest of the criminal crew will soon be returning to the warehouse. They must figure out a way to escape. But they struggle with how to live out the situation because each one is wondering if he is the kidnapper or the kidnapped.

Do I live as a criminal? Do I live as a police officer?

They don't know how to behave in the warehouse because they don't know who they are. During a struggle the main character says, "How do I know how to act when I don't even know who I am?"

Great question.

How do you know how to live if you don't know who you are?

God wants you to know exactly who you are in relation to the world around you. So that you will live out the reality of who you are in this world, God reminds you of your identity through the apostle Peter's letter:

> Dear friends, I urge you, as aliens and strangers in the world, to abstain from sinful desires, which war against your soul. Live such good lives among the pagans that, though they accuse you of doing wrong, they may see your good deeds and glorify God on the day he visits us.
> (1 Pet. 2:11–12 NIV)

Peter was writing a group of Christians who were struggling with how to live in this world. These Christians were experiencing intense persecution. They were hated. The root of the hostility toward them was the fire that burned Rome to the ground. The Roman culture was devastated. Careers were lost. Homes were burned. Families were ripped apart. People died. Life as they knew it was gone. It was a huge tragedy.

The Roman citizens wanted to blame someone. Anger and frustration needed to be directed toward someone. Initially the Romans believed that Nero, the Roman emperor, had set fire to his own city. He was suspected of the unthinkable act because of his insatiable desire to build new things. He loved building projects.

Nero responded by shifting the blame and hatred toward other people. He blamed you. He directed the blame toward Christians. He accused Christians of setting fire to the city; therefore, great hostility and persecution broke out against the Christians, not only in Rome but also all over the Roman Empire. Christians were spread and dispersed everywhere, and they were wondering how to live now in this world.

How do we know how to live when we don't know exactly how we fit?

Peter reminds us of our relationship to the culture, to the world around us. We must know who we are if we are going to live out the faith in our culture. We must understand who we are in relation to the world around us.

Where Do You Fit?

How do you view yourself in relation to the world around you?

Many people view this world as their home. And why not? They sleep, eat, play, work, commute, and live in this world. In their mind this world is where they fit. It is where they belong. Add some ambition, and we find the recipe for the world's version of success.

Several years ago a popular gang movie was based on the Miami drug scene. The movie *Scarface* has become iconic in our culture. In recent years a video game based on the movie was released. The name of the video game is "Scarface: The World Is Yours."

The world is yours.

The phrase comes from the movie. In the movie Tony Montano lived in a huge mansion. In the foyer of the mansion was a statue of the world and written on it was the phrase, "The world is yours." The message has been driven into our culture and reinforced through a new generation of cultural icons.

You belong here so make it big. Make as much money as you can. Watch out for number one. Go for yours. The world is yours.

The message is erroneous.

The world is not yours or mine. The world belongs to God. Actually, Scarface hijacked the classic line from the Scripture. God says, "The world and everything in it is Mine" (Ps. 50:12).

Ironically, at the end of the movie, Scarface is shot and killed. He falls dead into the pool underneath the statue. And all he collected in his brief life stayed behind. The world was not his.

While some people view this world as their home, others approach life through the lens of a dual citizenship. These people believe they belong to two worlds: God's kingdom and this world. There are two sets of friends, one for each world. And two sets of vocabularies, one for each kingdom. There are even two sets of finances; people pay taxes in this world and tithe in the kingdom of God.

If you view yourself as a dual citizen, you see no problems with inconsistencies in your life. After all, you belong in two places. You have a foot in each world. When you live and breathe in the Christian world, you speak that language and act a certain way. But when you are in the other world, you fully belong there as well.

If you are attempting to live as a dual citizen, the tension is eating away at your soul. Although you insist you can juggle the two worlds, you find yourself miserable in both. What is the reason for the tension and discomfort?

The Holy Spirit.

God is uncomfortable with the inconsistencies. And He lives within you. He has been there since the moment you became a Christian. He is with you all the time, and when He is uncomfortable, you will be as well. His discomfort and conviction is a reminder that you really belong to Him.

Some view this world as their home. Others approach life as a dual citizen. But how does God want us to view ourselves in relation to the world around us? According to the apostle Peter, we do not belong to this world. We do not even have dual citizenship, as if we belong to Christ and to this world.

We are aliens and strangers in this culture.

You are an alien. Since I live in Miami, I need to clarify: you are a legal alien.

Legal Aliens

In the original language, *alien* literally means you are someone who lives alongside the people who belong here.

You don't really belong. You're not part of the family. You live alongside the family, but you are not a member of the house. You don't have a key. You don't have a room in the house or a seat at the table. You are on the outside.

You are not a citizen here. You are a stranger in this world. You are a foreigner in this land because of your faith. Thus you feel awkward at times. You often sense you don't quite fit. Some people look at you like you are odd. You are odd. You belong to the kingdom of God, not the kingdom of this world.

Peter begs these Christians to live out their identity as aliens and strangers. "Dear friends, I urge you, as aliens and strangers in the world" (1 Pet. 2:11 NIV). Peter is pleading, "Please get this. Please live out the reality of your identity."

Why is Peter begging?

Remember, the world was watching these Christians to see how they lived. They were under a microscope. They were accused of starting the fire that burned Rome to the ground. People were looking for any inconsistency in the lives of these Christians.

So Peter begs them to abstain from sinful desires and to live a good life in front of people. He begs them to live with integrity, to do the right thing. People are accusing them of doing wrong, so they must overcompensate. They must live such a good life that people will notice their good deeds and glorify God.

Peter begs because the world is watching.

The world is still watching.

We can identify with Peter's begging, can't we? Because we know that nothing hurts the cause of Christ more than

Christians who do not live out their faith. Nothing hurts the movement of the gospel more than our failing to live what we say we believe. The Hindu leader Gandhi reportedly said, "I like your Christ. I do not like your Christians. Your Christians are so unlike your Christ."

I went to college in the buckle of the Bible Belt—North Louisiana. The Bible Belt is marked with churches on almost every corner. I became friends with a guy named Bryce in my sociology class at Louisiana Tech. He was a brilliant guy and extremely interesting to talk with. We shared lunch a few times, and the conversation moved toward faith. I shared with him my story, how Christ changed me.

Bryce told me he was agnostic before he came to school in North Louisiana.

He had grown up in a big city outside the culture of the Bible Belt. I was waiting for him to say that he was now open to faith, that he wanted to discuss what following Christ would mean for him. I was certain that being surrounded by the Christianity of the Bible Belt would soften his agnostic position. My heart sank as the conversation continued.

After being in the Bible Belt, he had become an atheist. He said, "After seeing all these so-called Christians, I know this cannot be real."

So I identify with Peter's plea. Abstaining from sin and living good lives differentiates us from the world around us. We are different and we must live differently.

Peter begins with who we are, with who you are. We are aliens and strangers. Why does Peter call you an alien? What makes you so different?

Different Leader ~ Christ

Countries, cities, and cultures are often characterized by their leader. Germany was marked by Hitler's dictatorship for a generation. The United States was dramatically impacted by Abraham Lincoln's leadership. New York City was redefined by Rudolph Giuliani's administration. And Cincinnati was marked by Jerry Springer's leadership as mayor. Umm, maybe not. For the sake of the 'Nati, let's hope not.

The kingdom of God is led by the Christ. You are a member of His kingdom; therefore, you follow His leadership. He is your king.

He became your leader when you became a Christian. A prerequisite for belonging to the kingdom of God is submitting your life to Christ as your Lord, your boss, and your leader (Rom. 10:9). You follow a different leader than those who are citizens of this world.

> For, as I have often told you before, and now
> say again even with tears, many live as enemies of
> the cross of Christ. Their destiny is destruction,
> their god is their stomach, and their glory is in
> their shame. Their mind is on earthly things. But
> our citizenship is in heaven. (Phil. 3:18–20 NIV)

People without Christ as their leader follow their own desires. Their god is their stomach. In other words they are their own god. They seek fulfillment, pleasure, and purpose in themselves instead of in God.

Our citizenship is in heaven, and our allegiance is to the King of that kingdom. As Christians, we submit to the authorities placed over us in this world, but our ultimate leader is Christ. We simply follow Him.

In the early days of Christianity, we were known as followers of the Way (Acts 9:2). We were later called Christians, which literally means "the Christ people" (Acts 11:26). We have always been recognized as people who followed Christ.

Christ's invitation to His disciples was simple and clear, "Follow Me." When Peter and Andrew responded to Christ's invitation, they dropped their fishing nets (Matt. 4:19–20). The dropping of their nets was symbolic of a quick farewell to their old way of life. They left their profession, their homes, their daily routine, and their families. They left everything to follow Christ.

Jesus never asked His disciples to follow a religious institution or denomination. He always insisted, "Follow Me." Being a Christian has always been about following Christ. The call to follow Him is not complicated. We simply lay down our nets and follow.

Unfortunately we often complicate and pollute the simplicity of the faith.

We often view Christianity as an institution to believe in or a creed to sign off on. Sadly we produce some Christian leaders who are more passionate about a particular doctrinal position than about Christ. In some circles following Christ has been reduced to believing the right information. We have confused information with transformation.

Do not misread me. Our beliefs are vital; they matter. God cares deeply what we believe about Him, but our beliefs should be reflected in our transformed lives. Being a disciple means *obeying* all that Jesus commanded, not just knowing His commands (Matt. 28:19). We are called to live the faith, not just hear it (James 1:22). We are invited to follow our leader in how we walk in this world, not just in what we believe (1 John 2:6).

You follow a different leader, and you obey a different law.

Different Law

People are accountable for the laws of the state or country where they reside. In some states there are some strange laws that amazingly are still on the books. Realizing that most laws are reactionary to specific situations makes the following laws hilarious.

For example, in Ohio it is illegal to get a fish drunk. In Washington it is against the law to attach a vending machine to a utility pole. In Texas it is illegal to sell one's eye. In New York you cannot walk around on Sundays with an ice cream cone in your pocket. In North Carolina it is illegal for elephants to be used to plow cotton fields.[1]

Humanity specializes in formulating laws.

Since we tend to be law oriented, we must guard against legalism in our faith. Because we have the God-given desire to differentiate ourselves from the world coupled with our proclivity to make laws, we have the tendency to develop a list of rules that mandates what separation from the world looks like.

The religious crowd in Jesus' day was notorious for their laws. The Pharisees made rules about where to walk, how to eat, what to wear, and what you could not lift or carry on the Sabbath. They utilized rules to prove themselves more holy than others.

Modern-day Pharisees pull out similar rules.

Maybe you have encountered some of the rules: Coed swimming is sinful. Playing spades with your parents is like playing cards with the devil himself. Good Christians don't listen to music with a beat. People who respect God dress a specific way at church. True believers read only a certain version of the Bible. Real worship occurs only with a certain musical style.

Setting up nonbiblical rules as essential reeks of pharisaical legalism. While the motivation may be differentiation from the world, the legislation of man-made rules displeases God (Mark 7:8). The end result of legalism is people who apparently obey God externally but are rotting internally. Jesus told the Pharisees they were walking coffins. On the outside they looked clean, but on the inside they were full of death (Matt. 23:27).

The law in the kingdom of God is unlike the law of the world. The law you obey is not a complicated list of rules and regulations. You submit to the law of the Spirit. "If you are led by the Spirit, you are not under the law" (Gal. 5:18).

As an alien in this culture, you should abstain from sinful desires (1 Pet. 2:11), but a list of rules does not give you the power to refrain. Religion is empty because it lacks the power of the Spirit. While the Holy Spirit will never lead you to violate the Word of God, His guidance eliminates the need for a list of regulations. People revert to religion for easy confirmation that they have done what is right, that they have checked off items on a list of dos and don'ts.

The law of the Spirit requires the discipline to seek God, the sensitivity to listen to His voice, and the faith to be led by Him. As an alien and stranger, you have a new law, which is simply to heed the language of the Spirit of God who lives within you.

Different Language

As an alien in this world, you hear a different language. Different cultures and countries speak and hear different languages. Cultures are often defined by their language. If you don't know the language, you don't belong.

Growing up in New Orleans in the South, I was raised saying *y'all.* How *y'all* doing? When I moved to the Midwest, I was roasted for saying *y'all.* To survive I learned to say *you guys.* Hey, how *you guys* doing? When I have spoken in Jersey or Philly, I have tried to acclimate to the culture by saying, *you's guys.* Actually pronounced *youz guyz.*

As a citizen of heaven, you hear the language of God's kingdom. You recognize His voice because you are His (John 10:27). You sense Him speaking and you understand. The tug on your heart, the nudge in your spirit—not everyone experiences that.

One night, early in my journey, I sensed His voice. I will never forget the night.

It was my senior year in high school, and I was struggling with how to live out my new relationship with God. I loved my friends so much, but I knew that God had changed my life and that I did not fit into this world any longer. But I tried hard to make it work. I was attempting to live as a dual citizen with one foot in this world and one foot in the kingdom of God.

I went to a club with some of my friends. We got into the club with our fake IDs. We were out on the dance floor. All of a sudden the song "Highway to Hell" roared through the speakers. The chorus kicked in. Everything seemed to be moving in slow motion. I looked around and saw all these people with their hands in the air, shouting *Highway to Hell* like they were celebrating.

Everything was quiet except for the song. And His voice.

You belong to Me now.

I sensed God speaking; I knew His language. I sensed His conviction.

I never felt so out of place in my life. I realized that I was an alien, a stranger in the room. I felt uncomfortable because I was supposed to feel uncomfortable. I was commanded to live alongside my friends, but there needed to be a difference in how I lived. The difference must be greater than the fact that I went to church a few hours every week.

As a citizen of heaven, you hear the language of God's kingdom. Throughout the day God is speaking. You see Him at work in your office, on your job site. You hear His voice not audibly but internally. You sense His presence on the way to work. You see His hand in creation on your vacations.

As a citizen of heaven and an alien in this world, you follow a different leader, obey a different law, and hear a different language. How should your identity impact how you live? How do you live out the reality of who you are? In light of our identity as aliens, the apostle Peter urges us to (1) hold back from sin and (2) live well among the people.

Hold Back from Sin

While we are on this earth, we will never eliminate sin. Sin wages a war against your soul. Temptation is going to be a constant struggle.

An eighty-five-year-old theology professor was speaking to his Bible college class. One of the young college students raised his hand to ask the professor a question. He asked, "At what age in life do you stop struggling with lust?" The professor thought for a moment and answered, "I am not sure. I know that it is some time after eighty-five."

Sadly some people constantly feel guilty because of temptation. They live defeated and discouraged lives because of the war. The enemy has convinced them that if they really love God they would not face temptations. I have talked with people who question their faith because of the temptations they face.

Your enemy, the devil, seeks to make you feel guilty and defeated about temptation so that you will quit fighting, so that you will lie down and give up. But temptation and sin are not synonymous.

We read about the temptation of Christ, not the sin of Christ. Jesus defeated every single temptation that came to Him. Jesus was and is completely sinless and pure. Jesus was tempted but He did not sin. If temptation and sin were the same, Jesus would have been unable to be the pure sacrifice for our sins.

Sin occurs when we surrender to temptation. Sin is saying *yes* when temptation comes to you. When an evil thought knocks on the door of your mind, that is not sin. Sin is when you invite the thought into your mind, sit down for dinner with the thought, and mull it over. When you find yourself in a situation where you are under temptation, you have not yet sinned. Sin occurs when you surrender to temptation.

Obviously we do not want to sin. Sin leaves us empty. Sin harms our relationship with God and hurts people in our lives. Moreover, sin displeases and disgusts God. But if temptation is not the same as sin, when does sin occur? How does sin happen?

> When tempted, no one should say, "God is tempting me." For God cannot be tempted by evil, nor does he tempt anyone; but each one is tempted when, by his own evil desire, he is dragged away and enticed. Then, after desire has conceived, it gives birth to sin; and sin, when it is full-grown, gives birth to death. (James 1:13–15 NIV)

An Equation for Sin

Sin is born in our lives when our desires are married to temptation. Our desires hook up with temptation, and our sinful desires get pregnant with sin. Sin is born, and when it grows up, death occurs. Sin that we allow to fester, sin that we allow to remain unchecked brings death. Sin destroys. Relationships suffer. Opportunities die.

The terms *dragged away* and *enticed* are hunting terms in the original language. Our own longing for temptation pulls us into sin. When a hunter seeks to trap an animal, the hunter uses the desires of the animal against him.

Our sinful desires pull us into temptation, and sin is born. Sin, unchecked and unconfessed in our life, brings pain and death. If there were a mathematical equation for sin, it would be: temptation + desire = sin.

To abstain from sinful desires and live as an alien in this culture, you must address both factors in the equation: temptation and desire. One of my mentors taught me if the desire is there, ask God to remove the opportunity, the temptation. If the opportunity or the temptation is there, ask God to remove the desire. You will not be perfect; you will not live sinless, but you can avoid the painful pattern of ongoing sin.

DON'T BE STUPID

Let's begin with the temptation side of the problem. Handle temptation with wisdom. Temptation is always going to exist, but be wise with it. Don't be an idiot. Do not place yourself in places where temptation strongly matches an area in which you struggle.

If you struggle with lust, do not place yourself in front of the Internet after your family or roommates go to bed. If you struggle with gossip, do not go to the breakfast meeting where you know you will be dragged into idle chatter. If you struggle with drunkenness, do not flip the menu over to the side where you will be tempted. If you struggle with anger, do not play church league basketball. If you struggle with gluttony, do not go to the Golden Corral buffet with sweatpants on. It is like one big horse trough.

You get the point. Be wise with temptation.

Jesus was wise with temptation. He only placed Himself in places God led Him to go. In the temptation story of Christ, God led Jesus into the desert (Matt. 4:1). Jesus was following God. He went where God led Him to go.

If you only place yourself in environments where God leads you to go, you will drastically lower the amount of temptation you face.

DEALING WITH DESIRE

Addressing the temptation side of the equation is insufficient however. You also must deal with your sinful desires. The answer is not to run off, live in the woods, and never associate with the rest of the world.

Throughout the history of Christianity, scores of people have been frustrated with the battle. To deal with the struggle of sin, some have sought to remove themselves from temptation. In the third century, groups of Christians moved to the desert in Egypt. They became known as the Desert Fathers, and they lived in complete isolation from the world.

Some reasoned that by removing themselves completely from the world that they would be able to overcome sin. However, their flight did not eliminate temptation and sin. Many struggled with envy or lust. Some wrote extremely depressing laments of their own depravity. In other words, they still struggled.

To abstain from sinful desires, you must live in the power of God. You must do more than avoid the bad stuff. You must walk with God in a growing and vibrant relationship. You must follow your King, obey the law of the Spirit, and listen to the language of the kingdom.

> So I say, live by the Spirit, and you will not
> gratify the desires of the sinful nature. For the sin-
> ful nature desires what is contrary to the Spirit,

and the Spirit what is contrary to the sinful nature. They are in conflict with each other, so that you do not do what you want. (Gal. 5:16–17 NIV)

The war is taking place inside you. Because the conflict is within, you are incapable of defeating temptation in your own strength and energy. It is impossible. When you fight the battle in your strength, you lose. But you have the power of God living inside you. When you became a Christian, the Holy Spirit of God moved into your life.

You have a choice. You can live in the power of the Spirit, or you can live in the power of your desires. Right now either you are surrendering control to the Holy Spirit, or you are surrendering control to your sinful desires.

An Indian who recently became a Christian described the inner conflict the best. The missionary who led the Indian to Christ went to visit him. The Indian was sitting in his teepee looking troubled. The missionary asked him what was wrong. The missionary was concerned. The Indian was a new Christian; why was he not more excited, more full of joy?

The Indian said that there was an inner battle. The missionary asked for explanation. The Indian said there are two dogs. *One dog is my God dog. He wants to do what is right.* The missionary realized that the Indian was describing the Holy Spirit. He simply used different wording. *The other dog is bad. He wants to do wrong.* The missionary was impressed. The Indian was describing the inner war.

The missionary asked, "Which dog is winning?"

The dog I feed the most.

If you are going to win the battle and abstain from sinful desires, you must feed the Holy Spirit that lives within you. How do you feed the Holy Spirit, the God dog?

Jesus, during His temptation, quoted Scripture. He prayed. He fasted.

And you must starve the sinful flesh. You will carry your flesh until you die, until you are in heaven. But you do not have to surrender to it. Starve it. Be wise with what you put in front of your eyes, with what you allow to enter your mind.

As an alien, abstain from your sinful desires and live a good life among those who don't know God.

Live Well among People

If we are actively growing in our faith, our lives will be visibly different. Sin will not corrupt and destroy our example. Our good deeds will be visible to the world around us. As we live righteously attractive lives, people will take note. People will see our lives, and they will glorify God.

We are to live differently. We are to live right. We are to live blameless and above reproach. But we are to do so *among the pagans,* among people who are far from God. We are challenged to abstain from sin, not to abstain from sinful people.

What is your response to the world around you? Do you live a godly life among people who are without Christ?

For centuries Christians have debated what our response to the world around us should be. During the 1940s, Yale professor Richard Niehbur gave a series of lectures on how Christians respond to culture. His lectures became a classic book entitled *Christ and Culture.* In the book, Niehbur explains five common Christian responses to the world around us. While my updating and brief take on the five common reactions to culture might differ somewhat from Niehbur's original lecture, I give him credit for providing a great framework for discussion.[2]

FIVE VIEWS

The first response to the world around us is *Christ above culture*. This view emphasizes that Christians are above the culture; therefore, they do not need to engage the culture. The *Christ above culture* view says, "We are better than you. Our way of life is better than yours. In fact, we are so above the culture that we should isolate ourselves from the world."

People who practice *Christ above culture* remove themselves as much as possible from the culture. The movie *The Village* is a good example. A group of people is disgusted with the culture. Each of them has been dramatically hurt by the world. The group decides to create their own village deep in the woods.

Although the residents of the village live in modern times, they re-create life from several centuries ago. They build their own homes, make their own clothes, raise their own food, and marry other villagers. They never leave the village. The totality of their lives is self-contained within the village.

To prevent their children from desiring to wander outside the village, the founding elders construct an elaborate story to keep their own from wandering off to "the towns." The people in the village have been led to believe that there are vicious creatures living in the woods surrounding the village. These creatures or "those we do not speak of" have agreed not to harm the people if they will stay within the confines of the village.

The elders of the village meant well. They wanted to protect their children from the pain of the world. However, the pain of the world is also found within the village. The villagers could not escape the depravity of humanity.

Many Christians live in a secluded village. They seek jobs with other Christians, spend several nights a week at church, place their kids in Christian little leagues, and only "fellowship" with other believers. They lay their heads on their pillows at night thanking God they lived another day unscathed by the world.

Village life is not the Christian life.

While those who disengage from the world believe they are obeying God, they are living the antithesis of the gospel and Peter's challenge. Christ came to this world, and Peter challenges us to live such good lives "among the pagans"—not removed from them.

The second response to the world is *Christ of culture.* People who adopt a *Christ of culture* view of the world believe that Christ is fully in the culture. He is in every thought. He is in every movie. He is in every conversation. He is in the strip club because God made the woman who is dancing. And He made the pole. God is in the Fergie song because He inspired all types of music. He is everywhere and in everything; you just have to open your eyes to see Him.

In conversations with dope heads, guys will insist God created marijuana for them to enjoy life. One even insisted God is in the weed so the more he smoked, the more he "got God in his lungs."

Yeah, dude.

Christ of culture sounds (and smells) a lot like pantheism: God is in all. He is in everything; therefore, Christians can embrace and enjoy the culture fully because Christ is there. While village living compromises the mission of Christ, those who practice *Christ of culture* violate the holiness of Christ (James 4:4).

The third response to our world is *Christ against culture.* People who are against the culture believe that God is continually mad at the culture. They insist they are on an assignment from God to attack the culture, to expose everything that is wrong with the context in which they live. They are similar to the *Christ above culture* group, but instead of choosing isolation they picket and protest.

The worst expression of *Christ against culture* is extremists who blow up abortion clinics in the name of God. The best expression is Christians who approach life as a battle with people who are not Christian. While the spiritual life is portrayed as a battle throughout Scripture, the battle is against our own desires and against the powers of darkness (Eph. 6:12), not against people. Unfortunately both the best and worst case scenarios are damaging. Instead of expressing love to people in the culture, the *Christ against culture* group expresses hatred and disgust.

The fourth response to the world is *Christ and culture in paradox,* or those who insist on maintaining dual citizenship. As we discussed earlier, people who insist they belong to this world *and* the kingdom of God live confused and inconsistent lives. During some moments they live as citizens of God's kingdom. At other moments they walk as citizens of the world. Their values change with their surrounding.

The fifth response to the world is *Christ transforming culture.* People in the *Christ transforming culture* perspective believe Christ seeks to transform the culture and specifically the people within the culture. This view of culture cares predominately about the hearts of people within the culture.

God desires for you to be a transformer of culture, to live a good life *among* people who do not know Him. Your life should be a statement of the gospel, a walking billboard of God's transforming power. And as people see your righteously attractive life, God will draw them to Himself.

My wife, Kaye, lives *Christ transforming culture*. She grew up in a small town with more cows than people but has gladly followed me to the cities where God has led us. In both Cincinnati and Miami, she sensed God urging her to teach in the public school system. She turned down very appealing Christian school offers (small class size and curriculum with a biblical worldview) to teach elementary kids in a public school.

Kaye does not preach the gospel. She lives the gospel . . . in front of people. She loves people, works hard, teaches with creativity and excellence, engages families relationally, humbly stands for what is right, and lives a life filled with joy and peace.

In time people are curious about the difference in her life. And because of the trusted relationship she has with people, she is granted the privilege to explain the hope that she has (1 Pet. 3:15).

In Cincinnati her team teacher was JoAnn Tiemann. JoAnn and Kaye loved to teach together because they both are creative, passionate for kids, and love to have fun. They quickly became great friends.

JoAnn was not a Christian. Not at first.

Kaye never condemned JoAnn for her lifestyle (*Christ against culture*), nor did she participate (*Christ of culture*). Kaye did not ask to be transferred to another teaching team (*Christ above culture*); she simply lived the gospel in front of JoAnn. She brought her best to the classroom, displayed integrity, loved JoAnn, and began to share with her why she was so different. Kaye was God's transforming presence in the life of JoAnn. JoAnn became a Christian, and her life has never been the same.

Today Kaye and JoAnn are still very close. After JoAnn became a Christian, she began volunteering with Kaye in our youth ministry in Cincinnati. She met one of my interns, Todd Breiner. Her name is now JoAnn Breiner, and they live in Miami where Todd serves as middle school pastor at our church.

God desires to utilize you to transform the lives of those you live among.

How do you know how to live in this world if you don't know who you are? Do you know who you are? Are you ready to live out your identity as an alien in the culture?

The reality: You are an alien in this world.

The response: Abstain from sin and live a good life among people.

Group Discussion Questions

1. How have you seen the movement of the faith hurt by Christians who do not live out their faith? Does this cause you to identify with Peter's urging?

    bad plles, denying, looking to lade god . Yes.

2. As an alien, you follow a different leader. Why do you think Jesus was so clear about the cost of following Him? Does it cost much to follow Him now? *To weed out people.* Sure, but its worth it.

3. As an alien, you hear a different language. Can you think of a time in your life when you know God was speaking to you? *Prom, Dan,*

4. If sin occurs when temptation and desire meet, what are some practical ways to address the temptation side of the equation? *Scripture, HS, Dont be stupid*

5. What are some practical ways to address the desire side of the equation? How do you feed the God dog? *Scripture, HS, Gods power, starve the crop flesh*

6. Which responses to culture do you feel are most prevalent? Which view do you tend to live by?

    Christ above culture. Christ against.

CHAPTER 8
||||||||||||||||||||||

You Are His Ambassador

(that you may declare)

*am·bas·sa·dor (noun): a diplomatic official
of the highest rank sent by a government to
represent it on a temporary mission*

W ait!
Stop. Don't turn the page yet.

I know what you are thinking. You think this chapter is
about witnessing or telling people about your faith. Perhaps
you read the word *ambassador* and thought of the word
evangelism.

This chapter is not about sharing your faith. Well, not exactly. This chapter is more about who you are than what you do.

When you realize you are an ambassador, how you approach people will change. When you understand you are an ambassador, how you approach life will change.

I know because things changed for me. I am a recovering Jesus salesman.

Share not tell

Jesus Salesman

At one point early in my faith journey, I thought that telling people about Jesus was a sales job. And that I was a salesman. A Jesus salesman. My job was to present Jesus to people in the most compelling way possible. My passion was to master the art of selling. I put a lot of pressure on myself to sell Jesus the right way.

My job was to say the right things at just the right times, to maximize opportunities when people would be most receptive. To sell Jesus the right way, I learned the right "transition statements" to move the conversation toward Christ. If someone did not buy Jesus, I failed. Perhaps I forgot to mention a verse that highlighted the benefits of becoming a Christian.

And like any good salesman, I had to close the deal.

If I could not close the deal, the rest of the sales call was meaningless. Closing the deal was the point of the conversation. And in my sales team network, closing the deal meant convincing people to pray a prayer where they would commit their lives to Christ. Once the magical prayer was prayed, the sales job was complete. The sales call often looked like this:

Do you want to escape frying forever in hell like a human sausage?

Do you want to have joy for the rest of your life?

Do you want meaning and purpose?

Then you need to try Jesus. Trying Jesus is easy. And free. But you need to decide now. The offer does not last long. All you need to do is tell Jesus you want to try him. I can help you. Just repeat after me . . .

I painfully remember one occasion when I lived the reality of my mistaken identity as a salesman. I was approaching the end of my senior year in high school. I was a new Christian and fired up to tell people about Jesus.

I was also interested in business, and a well-respected businessman in our community invited me to join him in Amway. No, I am not making this up. I joined and immediately started recruiting people to be in my organization. I was planning for six people in the first few months.

There was an Amway event in New Orleans, and I invited a guy from work to come with me. I picked him up at his house, and we drove into the city for the event. On the way I began to sell him on Jesus. And on Amway. I was more passionate for Jesus than Amway, but my approach felt the same. I closed the deal on Jesus, and he prayed and asked Christ into his life.

On the way home I tried to close the deal on Amway. He wanted more time to think about it. Unfortunately the story ends there.

I saw him at work for several more months but never talked to him about his faith. To be honest, I never thought about teaching him how to follow Christ after he expressed a desire to know God. I sincerely thought my work with him was done. I wanted to focus on new people I needed to convince.

Since I viewed myself as a Jesus salesman, my job was done when the deal was closed. Once someone would confess faith in Christ, I was successful.

I think about him now and hope he really did become a Christ follower. Maybe God used my foolishness. Perhaps his prayer to God was authentic and God brought someone else into his life to nurture him along the journey.

But I don't ever want to be a Jesus salesman again.

The more I read Scripture, the more I realize how big a commitment becoming a follower of Christ is. Jesus said, "If anyone would come after me, he must deny himself and take up his cross and follow me" (Mark 8:34 NIV). Inviting people to Christ is inviting them to die. Christ calls us to make disciples, not ask people to make a decision to try our product Jesus (Matt. 28:19).

Jesus is not a product we add to our lives. We don't sprinkle our lives with a little bit of Jesus to make everything taste better. He is God. When we become a Christian, He becomes our King.

Asking people to follow Christ is much deeper than a sales job. Jesus is much more than a product. And people are more important than potential customers.

As I went off to college, I left my identity as a salesman behind. I was convinced that my salesman identity was cheapening the gospel. I embraced a new identity, one that would lift high the value of complete commitment to Christ.

I became a hunter of heathens. . . .

Heathen Hunting

During my freshman year of college, I heard a preacher say that he and some friends went "heathen hunting." It sounded fun to me. Heathen hunting sounded radical and something I would enjoy doing with other passionate Christ followers.

I would not be a salesman anymore. I would hunt down heathens and tell them the whole truth about the gospel. I would confront firmly and confidently. I would go "all out" for the sake of the gospel.

As a freshman, I led a group of students at the college I attended to go door-to-door in dorms telling people about Jesus. Quoting Romans 1:16, I told other Christians that if they were not ashamed of Christ, they would join me on Tuesday nights. We would gather and talk about our experiences at the end of each night.

I began to feel uncomfortable when I heard people saying things like, "We got two people tonight" or "How many did you get?"

We were hunting for sure. But were the people we talked to real people to us? Did we care for them deeply? Or were they just notches on our spiritual hunting belts?

During my sophomore year of college, a group of my best friends and I decided the dorms were not daring enough. We were ready for big game hunting. We wanted to "target" some big prey. We needed a greater challenge. So we decided to go to the bars in our college town and tell people about Jesus.

On Monday nights we would barhop. Barhopping for Jesus was a badge of our boldness and unashamed commitment to the gospel. We entered bars, played pool, sat next to people, and went straight into the gospel. Not many people listened. But at least we were hunting.

One night during the prayer in the car, God convicted me. I will never forget the moment. One of my friends was praying and he prayed this:

> *Oh God. Thanks for giving us this opportu-*
> *nity to speak with boldness about You. Thank You*
> *that Your Word is a sword. I pray that we will take*
> *Your sword into this bar and just cut people up*
> *with it.*

Cut people up . . .

The rest of us started laughing hysterically during the prayer. It was a funny moment with some great friends. We got out of the car and went into the bar.

After we went home, I could not sleep. I had recovered from my spiritual salesman days, but was this approach any better? Being a hunter appealed to my desire to be a radical Christian, but was this what Jesus desired?

My view of myself impacted how I shared the gospel. Your view of yourself impacts how you share the gospel.

If you view yourself as a salesman, you will approach sharing the faith as a sales job. You will view people as potential customers. You will be eager to close the deal so you can accumulate a greater commission in heaven.

If you view yourself as an expert specialist on the faith, you will wait for people to approach you with their questions. You will live in your cocoon, constantly preparing for the questions you think will arrive. After all, you're the expert, and people will come to you to learn.

If you view yourself as a "God-warrior," you will seek to enter spiritual combat with people from the "dark side." Mrs. Perrin painfully lived the identity as a self-proclaimed God-warrior on an episode of the reality show *Trading Spouses*. Mrs. Perrin lived as the mom for this non-Christian family for a week. Unfortunately her identity as a God-warrior caused her to be unloving and joyless. She was unbearable and miserable to be around.

I cringed as I watched the episode. On AOL's home page the morning after the show aired, there was a big picture of Mrs. Perrin with the subheading: "If Mrs. Perrin is spending eternity in heaven, we would rather spend eternity with Satan." Sadly she typifies how Christians can be perceived in our culture.

A search on youtube.com for "God warrior" will give you a list of videos from the episode. Hundreds of people have commented on the videos. Here is a sampling of the comments:

> "Typical Christian. Irrational, hateful, domineering. Look how she terrorizes her own family and condemns anyone who doesn't worship her god." (Kathleen)
> "This is why I am an atheist." (Kingkong)
> "Take a good look people. This is what a TRUE Christian is. A self-centered, squealing pig who goes around condemning all to hell like she has the authority to do so." (Cassie)

Our understanding of our identity impacts how we share the good news of Christ with the world around us. If we do not possess a clear understanding of our identity, we might cheapen the gospel with salesman tactics. Or we might approach people in a harmful manner.

To influence the world around us, what identity has God given us? What view of ourselves does God desire us to adopt?

The Call to Be an Ambassador

God views you as His ambassador. The apostle Paul uses this language when writing to the Christians living in the city of Corinth:

> For Christ's love compels us, because we are convinced that one died for all, and therefore all died. And he died for all, that those who live should no longer live for themselves but for him who died for them and was raised again.
>
> So from now on we regard no one from a worldly point of view. Though we once regarded Christ in this way, we do so no longer. Therefore, if anyone is in Christ, he is a new creation; the old has gone, the new has come! All this is from God, who reconciled us to himself through Christ and gave us the ministry of reconciliation: that God was reconciling the world to himself in Christ, not counting men's sins against them. And he has committed to us the message of reconciliation. We are therefore Christ's ambassadors, as though God were making his appeal through us. We implore you on Christ's behalf: Be reconciled to God. God made him who had no sin to be sin for us, so that in him we might become the righteousness of God.
> (2 Cor. 5:14–21 NIV)

We have been reconciled to God. And now we have the message and the ministry of reconciliation. God wants to use us to bring people to Himself. In fact, God makes His appeal to people through us.

Through you.

You are an ambassador. An ambassador is a high-ranking dignitary with a major honor and responsibility. An ambassador represents his king and country in a different culture for a specific period of time.

You are Christ's ambassador. You belong to a different world (remember, you are an alien). Your citizenship is now in a different kingdom, but God has given you the honor to be His ambassador. You represent Christ and His kingdom in the culture where you live for a specific period of time.

Represent Christ

As an ambassador, your mission is to represent Christ. You stand for His kingdom while living in this one. You speak for Him. You love people on His behalf. You show compassion and mercy in His name. You stand for truth and justice as His representative.

God has given you a mission. Just as Jesus was sent to this world to rescue us, He has sent you to your world to rescue others (John 20:21). You have a mission.

Right now. Twenty-four hours a day.

The television show *24* is addictive to watch. Kaye and I refuse to watch *24* during the season because I cannot subject myself to the torture of a cliff-hanger every week. I have enough stress. I need resolution. So we wait until it comes out on DVD, and we vegetate around the TV for a few days.

Each episode of *24* is one hour in real time. So for an entire season, you are watching one day in the life of Jack Bauer. Jack Bauer is a renegade with the Counter Terrorism Unit. And each day he is on an exciting mission to save the world from terrorists. Jack's life is intense. Jack Bauer lives a life that counts, a life that is on mission. He knows exactly why he is on the planet. And his days, at least the six days I have seen, are exciting. They have meaning and purpose.

Secretly we long for a Jack Bauer kind of excitement in our days. We would love to be consumed with a mission that is worth fighting and even dying for. We think our days are boring in comparison.

Admittedly, if a camera followed us around for twenty-four hours, our day would appear very common. Even boring. We spend a lot of time in lines, in traffic, in bed, and in the mundane of life. The days and weeks pass, and we can feel pretty insignificant.

But as a Christian, each day is a mission. Your entire life is a mission trip. Each moment, you are an ambassador. And your mission is more important than Bauer's. Your mission is a matter of eternity, and your assignment is to represent Christ.

YOUR ASSIGNMENT

In a final conversation with His disciples, Jesus gives you your assignment. Jesus has been crucified and has been raised from the dead. He is about to ascend back to heaven. So in His last conversation with His disciples, He wants to be sure they understand the assignment.

So when they had come together, they asked Him, "Lord, at this time are You restoring the kingdom to Israel?"

He said to them, "It is not for you to know times or periods that the Father has set by His own authority. But you will receive power when the Holy Spirit has come upon you, and you will be My witnesses in Jerusalem, in all Judea and Samaria, and to the ends of the earth." (Acts 1:6–8)

Notice the disciples are asking Jesus when He will set up His kingdom on earth. They want to engage Him in a theological discussion about the end of time. Jesus essentially says they should not get caught up in the times and dates. Instead there is a mission to focus on.

Jesus says, "You *will* be My witnesses."

He does not say that you *might* be My witnesses or that one day you will *become* My witnesses. He does not say if you go to Bible school or take some classes on telling people about Me, then you will be My witnesses. When you receive the Holy Spirit, you are His witness. The moment you became a Christian, you became His ambassador.

But you do not live as His ambassador in your own power. You have the power of the Holy Spirit for the mission. The word *power* in the original language is *dunamis,* from which we derive the word *dynamite.* You have dynamite power from the Holy Spirit to live out your identity as an ambassador.

In fact, Jesus ties the giving of the Holy Spirit with the reality that you are His witness. One of the reasons He has given you His Holy Spirit is for the mission. Jack Bauer may have Chloe for his mission (and the ability never to use the bathroom), but you have the dynamite power of the Holy Spirit.

Jesus tells His disciples that they will first be witnesses in Jerusalem. Jerusalem is where they lived, ate, worked, and played. In the same way you represent Christ in your neighborhood, workplace, community, grocery store, mall, and fitness club. You represent Christ where you live, work, and play.

In His sovereignty God placed you in the house, condo, or apartment where you live. He planned for you to be there so you may be a transforming presence in the lives of people. He strategically placed you there as His ambassador.

In God's providence He placed you in your job. You are there for a much greater purpose than making money or succeeding in your career. God placed you there as His representative. The people working beside you, the ones in the cubicle next to you, or in the office down the hall have been divinely appointed to cross your path.

You have a mission in your day-to-day life; therefore, the mundane stuff of life matters. Every moment of your life has significance because the moments provide you opportunities to be a transforming presence in the lives of people.

When you understand your mission, the ordinary becomes sacred.

Every detail of your life is sacred because you represent Christ. The dull moments in your day are spiritual because of your identity as an ambassador. In fact, God uses the ordinary moments in your life to fulfill His extraordinary plan.

In the ordinary moments you are the aroma of Christ (2 Cor. 2:15). The joy and peace you bring to the office is sacred. People smell something different in your life. And it's not the new cologne or perfume you got for your birthday.

In the details of your day, you are the salt of the earth (Matt. 5:13). The example you set by bringing your best to your profession is sacred. You preserve the environment in which God has placed you. And people recognize the difference your presence makes.

In the mundane of life, you are the light of the world (Matt. 5:16). Your friendliness and patience with the cashier is sacred. Your goodness to others is attractive. People take notice, and they glorify God because of you.

Your relationship with your neighbors is sacred. Your consistent friendliness, honesty, and good deeds stand out like stars in the universe. They take note of you because you shine brightly in a world that is corrupt (Phil. 2:14–15).

The ordinary is sacred if you embrace your identity as an ambassador. Each moment is holy if you understand your calling. You have opportunities right where God has placed you to represent Him and to speak for Him.

I know this biblically, but I learned this watching three construction guys turn their job sites into sacred mission fields. They took me to school. . . .

CONSTRUCTION SEMINARY

The summer before I went to college, I worked construction in South Louisiana. I was one of the few Christians in the construction company. Duke, Denny, and Gary were three passionate Christ followers who taught me more than I learned in many seminary classrooms.

Each of us worked on a different job site, and we would meet together for prayer, Bible study, and lunch in the tool room. Actually, everyone else in the construction company called the tool room "the chapel." We were sometimes ridiculed for our faith. Once the tool room was trashed and "666" was painted all over the walls.

I watched as Duke, Denny, and Gary consistently loved and served the guys who ribbed them because of their faith. I watched how they worked hard and earned the favor of the supervisors. I watched how they always arrived at work the same way, on time and full of joy. I watched as they willingly and lovingly engaged people in conversations about Christ.

They viewed their job sites as a mission field. They were passionate for the people they worked alongside. Each day in the tool room/chapel, they would pray for people with whom they were sharing Christ on their job site.

The whole summer we prayed that people would come to know Christ. I wanted to see people get saved so badly. I thought that by seeing someone cross the line of faith, the persecution would be validated. But no one became a Christian that summer. And I went off to college.

A year and a half later, I visited my family at our home in New Orleans. I went to an event at a church, and I saw Duke. I was so excited to see him again. We hugged and I looked behind him.

Standing behind Duke was a guy from the scaffolding crew, one of the biggest and baddest dudes in the whole crew. You don't mess with the guys from the scaffolding crew. These guys were tough.

I will never forget Duke's words to me: "Eric, this is our new brother in Christ. He became a Christian a few months ago. We cannot even fit in the chapel anymore because so many guys are getting saved."

I learned so much from my construction worker friends. They knew they were more than construction workers. They were ambassadors. They realized their profession was more than a way to make money; it was a mission. They embraced the challenge to represent the King on their job. They viewed their days as sacred endeavors because of the opportunity to represent the kingdom of God while living in this foreign land.

As ambassadors, we are to represent Christ in the culture.

In the Culture

The Gospel of Matthew gives us a picture of how Jesus approached the culture surrounding Him. In Matthew 9 Jesus earns the title "friend of sinners."

> As Jesus went on from there, he saw a man named Matthew sitting at the tax collector's booth. "Follow me," he told him, and Matthew got up and followed him. While Jesus was having dinner at Matthew's house, many tax collectors and "sinners" came and ate with him and his disciples. When the Pharisees saw this, they asked his disciples, "Why does your teacher eat with tax collectors and 'sinners'?" On hearing this, Jesus said, "It is not the healthy who need a doctor, but the sick. But go and learn what this means: 'I desire mercy, not sacrifice. For I have not come to call the righteous, but sinners.'" (Matt. 9:9–13 NIV)

The story begins with Jesus finding Matthew sitting at the tax collector's booth. Tax collectors were the most despised people in the Jewish culture. They were worse than the IRS. They were known as traitors and thieves. They were traitors because they worked for Rome against their own countrymen, the Jews. They taxed their own people for the Roman government. They were thieves because they could tax people at their discretion to make their own pockets fat with coin.

Jewish history tells us that there were three types of publicans or tax collectors. There were the *gabbai*, or the general tax collectors, who collected taxes on property and land. There were the *great mokhes* and the *small mokhes*. *Mokhes* taxed people on anything and everything: cattle, children, servants, fish, boat, anything. The difference between the *great mokhes* and the *small mokhes* is that the *great mokhes* farmed out the collection process to others. They maintained some anonymity. No one really knew who they were.

The *small mokhes* were known. Everyone recognized them as tax collectors. They came to you and took your money anytime. Anywhere. While the *gabbai* and the *great mokhes* were hated, the *small mokhes* were despised the most. People, especially the religious, shunned these people. Matthew, because he was sitting in the tax collector's booth, was a *small mokhe*. He regularly took money from people.[1]

And this is the person Jesus asked to be His disciple.

When Jesus called him, Matthew got up and followed. Jesus did more than tolerate a tax collector. Jesus did not merely go on a once-a-year mission trip to see a tax collector.

Jesus not only preached to or at a tax collector. Jesus asked a tax collector to follow Him, to live with Him.

So what does Jesus do next with Matthew?

Jesus does not tell Matthew, "From now on you are never to be with or near a tax collector." He does not instruct him to live a life of isolation. Nor does He tell Matthew to picket and debate his former tax collector friends.

Instead, Jesus goes to a party with Matthew.

And because Matthew is a new believer, the other people at the party are "sinners and tax collectors"; thus, the beginning of Jesus' reputation as a "friend of sinners." The religious leaders felt that Jesus spent time with the wrong kinds of people, the people who drank too much, woke up in the wrong bed, and lived far from God.

The Pharisees, who bragged about their ability to isolate themselves from the world, could not believe that Jesus was having dinner with sinners and tax collectors. So they confront Jesus about His friendships. Of course, they don't actually go to Jesus directly. It is easier to go behind His back. The Pharisees ask His disciples, "Why does your teacher eat with sinners and tax collectors?"

Jesus hears the question and steps in. He says, "It is not the healthy who need a doctor but the sick. I have come to call sinners to Myself." The reason I am here is for them. The reason I am on the planet is for them.

So what was Jesus' relationship with the culture?

He did not compromise who He was. He lived a sinless and perfect life. Yet He did not isolate Himself from people. Jesus was called a friend of sinners because He deeply loved people who were on the outside of the kingdom of God. He was preoccupied with them. He longed to see people come to faith and live forever.

Jesus sought to transform the lives of people. Jesus did not seek to transform the political, legal, or religious scene of His day. He walked into a polluted political and religious system, and He did not address it. He did not attempt to transform the systems; He chose to transform the lives of people. All of the economic, religious, and political structures will one day crumble, so Jesus went after the hearts of people in the culture.

He lived among people. In the culture.

OUR DANGEROUS SUBCULTURE

You cannot be an ambassador if you avoid the world around you. You cannot be an ambassador if you spend the majority of your free time in a church building. Avoiding people within the culture is the antithesis of being an ambassador.

While the opposite should be true, research shows that the longer we are Christians the more we lose contact with people who do not have a relationship with God. We shell up and isolate ourselves from the world. We have built our own Christian subculture; and if we are not careful, we choose to live in it.

Living in our own subculture is easy to do. We have a Christian equivalent for everything. We have Christian radio, Christian bookstores, Christian record labels, Christian fitness centers, Christian schools, a Christian version of youtube.com (Godtube.com), Christian coffeehouses, Christian clubs, Christian wrestling teams, and even Christian theme parks. Our subculture makes it easy to live safe and content in a spiritual bunker.

Our Christian subculture may feel safe, but it is dangerous.

Our Christian subculture is dangerous because it can give us an excuse to disobey God. It can give us an excuse to disengage from people God has called us to engage and transform. It is dangerous because it has the potential to hurt the mission. It is dangerous because of the busyness it offers.

When I worked alongside Dr. Thom Rainer on the research and writing for *Simple Church*, my heart broke over the reality that many churches unintentionally hurt the advancement of the gospel. Many churches keep their people so busy doing church activities that they never have time to be friends with people who are far from God. Some Christians in our churches who can spend their entire lives without ever developing friendships with people who are "sinners and tax collectors."

Is this the kind of Christianity Jesus had in mind?

During the research I talked with church members in churches that are extremely busy. I met members who attend three to four Bible studies a week to become "better disciples." But they never spend time with people who are separated from a relationship with God.

Is this really discipleship?

Sadly we have often equated knowledge with discipleship. Thus our churches are filled with Bible study junkies who crave another hit or snort of curriculum knowledge but whose lives rarely reflect Christ. In the midst of all our knowledge, many neglect to relate to people who are far from God.

Please do not misunderstand me. I love the Bible. I study the Bible. I believe it is fully true, perfect, and pure.

I believe the Bible is essential for our growth and godliness. But should not all of our Bible studies and knowledge lead us to be more like Christ? If we were really being transformed, would we not have God's heart for people who are far from Him?

Jesus was accused of being a friend of sinners. Is being a friend of sinners a part of discipleship? When will someone give us that title?

As ambassadors, we are to represent Christ in the culture for a specific period of time.

For a Specific Period of Time

An ambassador is on a mission from his country of origin for a specific period of time. As an ambassador, you are here on this planet for a predetermined amount of time. And then the mission is over. Your time on this planet is the one shot, the one opportunity you have to represent Christ to people who do not know Him.

The brevity of our opportunity should create a sense of urgency.

The opportunity to be an ambassador for Christ will not last forever because our life is a vapor, here today and gone tomorrow (James 4:14). The Gospel of Mark tells the story of four guys who passionately brought a paralyzed man to Jesus. They lived their mission with a sense of urgency.

A few days later, when Jesus again entered Capernaum, the people heard that he had come home. So many gathered that there was no room left, not even outside the door, and he preached the word to them. Some men came, bringing to him a paralytic, carried by four of them. Since they could not get him to Jesus because of the crowd, they made an opening in the roof above Jesus and, after digging through it, lowered the mat the paralyzed man was lying on. When Jesus saw their faith, he said to the paralytic, "Son, your sins are forgiven." Now some teachers of the law were sitting there, thinking to themselves, "Why does this fellow talk like that? He's blaspheming! Who can forgive sins but God alone?" Immediately Jesus knew in his spirit that this was what they were thinking in their hearts, and he said to them, "Why are you thinking these things? Which is easier: to say to the paralytic, 'Your sins are forgiven,' or to say, 'Get up, take your mat and walk'? But that you may know that the Son of Man has authority on earth to forgive sins. . . ." He said to the paralytic, "I tell you, get up, take your mat and go home." He got up, took his mat and walked out in full view of them all. This amazed everyone and they praised God, saying, "We have never seen anything like this!" (Mark 2:1–12 NIV)

Jesus is talking to a huge crowd crammed in and around Peter's house. People begin to look up, as there is a loud noise on the roof. Peter is especially concerned. His house is being trashed, and the crowd far exceeds the fire code.

Jesus continues speaking, and then the noise begins again. A tiny hole in the roof appears. Debris starts falling. More noise, more debris. The hole gets bigger, and light begins to shine through. Then an entire section of the roof is ripped off. Peter must be livid. *What is going on? Who is on my roof? This is not right.*

Four guys appear looking through the hole. Just as people start to wonder what these guys are doing, they begin to lower their paralyzed friend to Jesus on a mat.

Surely these four unnamed guys first tried more conventional ways to get the paralyzed man to Jesus. Perhaps they attempted to go through the front door, but it was completely packed with people. They probably approached a window, but people were stacked five or six deep.

They could have said they tried. They could have gone home and told their friends how much they tried to bring someone to Christ. They could have wrapped up in prayer and returned to their families. But they persisted.

Homes in Palestine typically had flat roofs with a staircase on the side of the house. People would sit on top of the roofs to enjoy some cool night air. So these guys made their way to the roof. Perhaps they saw some of Peter's fishing ropes on the side of his house and tied the portable bed to the ropes.

I am sure they debated tearing up Peter's roof. After all, Peter was a little impetuous and loud-mouthed at times. But their love for their friend compelled them. They began to dig a hole in the roof. The original language literally says they "unroofed the roof." They dug through the thatch made of leaves, mud, and mortar. They destroyed the roof so they could lower their friend to Jesus.

Jesus said to the paralyzed man, "Son, your sins are forgiven." The words Jesus spoke were beautiful. He called him *Son*. He expressed friendship and love to him. He declared his sins to be forgiven.

While I love the story, I wonder how I would have acted that day.

How would you have responded to the situation, to the paralyzed man in need of Christ? Where would you fit in the story?

YOUR PART IN THE STORY

There was the crowd. They filled the room and surrounded the house to see Jesus. They stood and listened to Him speak. They watched as four people attempted to bring a paralyzed man to Jesus.

They watched.

Why did they not move out of the way? Why didn't they help? They were selfish. They were at Peter's house for a show. They wanted to see what Jesus would do and hear what Jesus would say. They were there first, and they were not giving up their spots.

The crowd missed an opportunity to be a part of bringing the paralyzed man to Jesus because they were not looking for the opportunity. They could have jumped in and helped. They could have brought some afflicted people from the town to Jesus, but evidently this did not even cross their minds.

Are you like the crowd, neglecting opportunities to bring people to Christ? Do you miss out because you are not looking?

The religious people are also in the story. Evidently they arrived early because they are the only ones sitting. They arrived early to critique. They evaluated the work of God rather than participate in it. They came into the house not with open hearts but with critical hearts. They united on criticism instead of uniting on the mission of bringing the paralyzed man to Christ.

Religious Christians are notorious for criticizing other Christians who are coloring outside the lines and breaking through roofs in attempts to bring people to Jesus. Are you like the religious in the story? Do you evaluate God's work or participate in it?

In the story we also see the four unnamed heroes, regular guys who were willing to take risks to bring someone to Christ. Their hearts were broken and burdened for their friend. The paralyzed man was most likely placed alongside the road to beg for money, but he was not left along the road.

Like the apostle Paul, the four guys' passion for the paralyzed man's redemption was greater than their concern for themselves (Rom. 9:1–3). So they took a risk. With urgency they busted up the roof.

Living the reality of your identity as an ambassador will cause you to take risks. Are you willing to break up a roof to get someone to Christ? Are you willing to risk your reputation at work to represent Him well? Are you ready to speak on His behalf?

The mission is temporary. And it requires some risk. You only have one life to make an impact. Are you ready to live the mission as His ambassador?

The reality: You are His ambassador.

The response: Represent Christ in the culture.

Group Discussion Questions

1. What have been your experiences with "witnessing" or sharing your faith with others?

Jake, On the streets, Kids

2. How does being an ambassador differ from
   common views of witnessing? *Showing not telling*

3. How could the ordinary aspects of your life be
   sacred opportunities to represent Christ?
   example of Christs...
   to small talk
4. How is the Christian subculture beneficial to *or big things!*
   us? (Like this cool book!) How is the Christian
   subculture harmful of the movement of the faith?
   Fellowship brings strength, Pushs people away
   tgroth
5. Jesus was known as a friend of sinners. If He were
   born in our culture, where would He spend His
   time? Who would He hang out with?
   Bars, Clubs, Public schools,

6. Read Mark 2:1–12 as a group. Who do you line up
   with the most: (1) the crowd, (2) the religious, or
   (3) the four guys? *The crowd*

7. How does busyness hurt our identity as
   ambassadors?
   Keeps our focus off the mission

CHAPTER 9
||||||||||||||||||||||

The Ending

*That you may declare the praises
of him who called you out of darkness
into his wonderful light.*

—1 PETER 2:9 NIV

Understanding who you are is essential. You are His child, the priest, the bride of Christ, His servant, God's friend, an alien, and an ambassador. These are more than fancy descriptions or titles. These are the reality of who God has made you to be. God has given you a new and great identity.

Your identity is from God. And your identity is for God. Your identity begins with God. And your identity ends with God.

The Beginning

Your great identity is from God, not from yourself. God is the author of your identity. Your identity began with His mercy extended toward you. Let's return to the central passage in the book:

> You are a chosen people, a royal priesthood, a holy nation, a people belonging to God, that you may declare the praises of him who called you out of darkness into his wonderful light. Once you were not a people, but now you are the people of God; once you had not received mercy, but now you have received mercy. (1 Pet. 2:9–10 NIV)

Now you have received mercy.

Mercy flows from God's nature. We see the mercy of our God early in the story. God created Adam and Eve and put them in a beautiful garden called Eden. Everything was perfect because sin had not yet entered the world and distorted everything. Adam and Eve walked with God and enjoyed perfect harmony with God and each other.

God told Adam and Eve that they could eat from any tree other than the *tree of knowledge.* If they ate from the *tree of knowledge,* they would know good and evil. They disobeyed God and ate from the *tree of knowledge.* God displayed His justice by judging their disobedience. God cursed the ground, and work became hard. God's judgment of sin brought the pain, death, and despair that we face every day.

But God also displays His mercy.

Sometimes we miss the mercy side of the story.

Adam and Eve realized their nakedness. They came to the knowledge of right and wrong and good and evil. They no longer benefited from the gift of being naïve.

But in a tangible and real way, God shows mercy.

> The LORD God made garments of skin for Adam and his wife and clothed them. And the LORD God said, "The man has now become like one of us, knowing good and evil. He must not be allowed to reach out his hand and take also from the tree of life and eat, and live forever." So the LORD God banished him from the Garden of Eden to work the ground from which he had been taken. After he drove the man out, he placed on the east side of the Garden of Eden cherubim and a flaming sword flashing back and forth to guard the way to the tree of life. (Gen. 3:21–24 NIV)

God made Adam and Eve garments. He met them at their point of shame and clothed them. He could have said, "Go find some leaves if you want." Instead He fashioned them clothes in the garden and dressed them.

But what about the suspension from the garden? How is that mercy?

When I read of their banishment from the garden, I think of being suspended from school. During the first week of seventh grade, I stole a bunch of padlocks off lockers throughout the school. They were not yet locked, so I took them off lockers, and I brought them home.

I learned how to hold the padlock close to my ear and listen for the faint click to discover the combination. I sold the padlocks and the combinations for half the price the school office was selling the combinations. Someone ratted me out, and I was called to the office. My father was waiting there with the assistant principal. And I was banished from school for a few days.

My suspension was an act of justice. My sinful deeds led to justice. And I received more justice when I got home that afternoon.

But Adam and Eve's expulsion from the garden was an act of mercy. God removed them from the garden and blocked the way to the garden of Eden so they could not eat from the *tree of life* (different from the *tree of knowledge*) and live forever. If Adam and Eve had eaten from the *tree of life*, they would have lived forever in a sinful and decaying body. Eternal life was not intended to be lived in decaying bodies.

God was displaying His mercy. And He has displayed His mercy in your life.

As He fashioned clothes for Adam and Eve to cover their shame, God has clothed you in His righteousness despite your sinfulness. And in His mercy God gave you a new identity, a great identity. He made you His child, the priest, the bride, His servant, God's friend, an alien, and an ambassador.

Your identity began with God.

And your identity ends with God.

The Ending

Your identity is from God and results in God being glorified. The end result of understanding your identity is that Christ is praised. The end result of knowing who you are in Christ is that you will honor and glorify God.

Look again at the apostle Peter's reminder.

> You are a chosen people, a royal priesthood, a holy nation, a people belonging to God, *that you may declare the praises* of him who called you out of darkness into his wonderful light. (1 Pet. 2:9 NIV, emphasis added)

That you may declare the praises . . .

Ultimately God has given you your great identity so that you will declare His praises. And not only with your lips but with your life. You honor God by living the reality of your identity.

- You declare His praises when you trust Him as your Father.
- You declare His praises when you enter His presence as the priest.
- You declare His praises when you live pure as the bride.
- You declare His praises when you serve as His servant.
- You declare His praises when you enjoy God as His friend.
- You declare His praises when you live differently as an alien.
- You declare His praises when you represent Christ as His ambassador.

Will you live the reality of who God has made you to be? Because of the beginning (God's mercy), will you live out the ending (God's glory)?

Live the ending.

Notes

Chapter One

1. William R. Yount, *Created to Learn: A Christian Teacher's Introduction to Educational Psychology* (Nashville: Broadman & Holman Publishers, 1996), 65.

2. Kenneth Boa, *Conformed to His Image: Biblical and Practical Approaches to Spiritual Formation* (Grand Rapids: Zondervan, 2001), 107.

3. Chip and Dan Heath, *Made to Stick: Why Some Ideas Survive and Others Die* (New York: Random House, 2007), 112.

4. Joshua W. Green and Shiva Kumar, *Witness: Voices from the Holocaust* (New York: The Free Press, 2000), 119.

Chapter Two

1. Augustine, *Confessions* (New York: Penguin, 1961).

2. Statistics from the National Fatherhood Initiative (www. fatherhood.org).

3. Louie Giglio, "Seeing God as a Perfect Father" (message series available at Northpoint resources: http://resources.north point.org).

Chapter Three

1. Justin Heckert, "I'm with the Steelers," *ESPN Magazine* (7 May 2007), 103.
2. Josephus, *Antiquities* Xv.11.5.417.
3. John MacArthur, *Hebrews* (Chicago: Moody Press, 1983), 225.
4. Gene Weingarten, "Pearls before Breakfast," *The Washington Post* (8 April 2007), W10.

Chapter Four

1. Malcolm Gladwell, *The Tipping Point* (New York: Little, Brown and Company, 2000), 153.
2. John MacArthur, *James* (Chicago: Moody Press, 1998), 208.

Chapter Seven

1. For more dumb laws, see www.dumblaws.com.
2. Richard H. Niebuhr, *Christ and Culture* (New York: Harper and Row, 1951).

Chapter Eight

1. John MacArthur, *Matthew 8–15* (Chicago: Moody Press, 1987), 61.

Biography

Eric Geiger serves as one of the vice presidents at LifeWay Christian Resources, leading the Resources Division. He received his doctorate in leadership and church ministry from Southern Seminary. He serves as the senior pastor of Clearview Baptist Church in Franklin, Tennessee. Eric authored or coauthored several books including the best-selling church leadership book, *Simple Church*.

Eric is married to Kaye, and they have two daughters: Eden and Evie. During his free time, Eric enjoys dating his wife, playing with his daughters, and shooting basketball.